beautiful everydays

A guide to living in the here and now

PALAK DAVE & LAURA L. BENN

Beautiful Everydays: A Guide to Living in the Here and Now
Copyright © 2024 by Palak Dave and Laura L. Benn

All rights reserved. No part of this publication may be reproduced, stored in a retrieval system or transmitted in any form or by any means, mechanical, electronic, photocopying, recording, scanning or otherwise - except for brief quotations in reviews or articles - without the prior written permission of the authors.

This book and any associated materials, suggestions and advice are intended to give general information only. Any likeness to real people or events mentioned in this book is purely coincidental. The authors expressly disclaim all liability to any person arising directly or indirectly from the use of, or for any errors or omissions in this book. The adoption and application of the information in this book is at the readers' discretion and is their sole responsibility.

Cataloguing in publication information is available from Library and Archives Canada.

ISBN 978-1-7382147-0-9 (hardback)

Published by Embiria Inc.

Copyedited by Courtney McAllister
Cover and interior design by Heeler Design
Photography by © Gooseberry Studios
Photo styling by Palak Dave and Laura L. Benn
Palak's author photograph by Katie Harrison

Discover the beauty
in simplicity.

everydays [noun]

We define everydays as those common, simple, ordinary and often overlooked happenings that in hindsight are the magical building blocks responsible for crafting a treasured lifetime. Although a daily occurrence, everydays are precious moments that can pass by in the blink of an eye, unless one slows down to enjoy and acknowledge their beauty.

For the home-lovers and dreamers,
Magic seekers and believers,
For those who crave stillness and imagination;
This book is your invitation
To step back into a simpler time
Where embracing everydays is a way of life.

contents

01   Foreword
02   A Gentle Guide

nest

08   Café at Home
16   Mood Lighting
22   Hideaway Nook
30   Heartfelt Decor
38   Personal Spa Day
46   Keepsake Box
52   Basket of Cozy
58   Wake Up + Wind Down Rituals

nourish

64   Brunch in Bed
70   Beautiful Boards
76   Time to Toast
82   Pretty Plating
88   The Art of Tea
96   "Just Because" Cake
102   Themed Meals
108   An Ode to Cookies

nurture

- 114 Escape into Books
- 120 Meaningful Playlist
- 126 Playtime with Pup
- 134 Emotional Painting
- 140 Moments with Water
- 146 All Dressed Up
- 154 Thoughtful Notes
- 162 More Ways to Celebrate

nature

- 168 Dining Al Fresco
- 174 Rainy Day Wander
- 182 Blooming Potential
- 188 Indoor Herb Garden
- 194 "Anywhere" Picnic
- 202 Propagating Plants
- 208 Magical Stargazing
- 216 Random Acts of Kindness

- 218 Closing Letter
- 222 Acknowledgments
- 226 Authors' Page

foreword

If only there was a way to bring a little more dreaminess to our day-to-day life. If only we could escape the frantic go-go-go nature of our modern world more often without an expensive vacation or a well-planned retreat. If only we could find a way back to a slower and simpler time.

We believe that all of the above is possible when we rediscover what we have, here and now, in new and nostalgic ways. We created this book to help guide that discovery.

The concept came to life years ago in a quaint café over our mutual love of cookies. Our conversation swirled around craving a deeper connection to our own lives and we wondered how we could make this simple, yet indulgent, afternoon the norm rather than the exception in our seemingly hectic schedules.

We wanted more calm, more beauty, more play and more time spent offline in meaningful ways. There had to be a way, some secret we weren't privy to.

Over time, we realized that there is no grandiose formula. We already had all we needed to make the magic happen, it was just a matter of rekindling it. The key, if you want to call it that, is learning how to embrace the everydays.

We started exchanging ideas, inspired by our childhoods – our younger, carefree days and our hopes for the future – to make each passing week a little more memorable and beautiful without adding another pressurized 'to do' item to our calendars. Soon we had an entire library of easy, dreamy activities that we could tap into at a moment's notice – and we'd like to gift them to you.

Each of the four sections of this guidebook – Nest, Nourish, Nurture and Nature – is about finding more offline enjoyment in all areas of your life and a deeper appreciation for the little things. And as a whole, this book is meant to show you a way towards the simpler life that you want, but can never find time for.

Welcome to *Beautiful Everydays* – your very own "cookbook" filled with recipes to create a life you love in the here and now. We hope you enjoy where these pages take you.

a gentle guide

There is no right nor wrong
Everything in this book is a suggestion. We've pulled together passions, practices, traditions and experiences from our own personal lives in hopes that you'll take them and make them your own. It's not about doing exactly as we say. It's not about following an exact formula for a precise result.

It's about using this book as a springboard for your own everydays and tapping into a feeling that transports you to a world of memorable possibility. It's about allowing yourself to try something new, to colour outside of the lines and to do so for no other reason than the pure delight of it all.

Unplug from everything
We mean everything.* Close your laptop, turn off the TV, hide your phone in a drawer – truly embrace being offline. Spend a little time getting lost in these pages, take some of these concepts out for a spin and disappear for a bit into a nostalgic way of living without the disruption of a screen.

Well, we mean almost everything. Music can be an exception because it brings such a beautiful mood to things.

Be open to playful messiness
Nothing squashes fun more swiftly than the unspoken pressure of expectation. More often than not we end up run down by the idea of doing it (whatever it is) "perfectly" and as a result any possibility for happiness evaporates before it really even has a chance to take shape. Repeat after us: "Messy is beautiful."

You are allowed to let go of expectations, to welcome play and wonder into your life. Doing so will help you to start seeing beauty in the most imperfect, messy, haphazard, all over the place things.

Slow down
This isn't a book to power through in the name of self-improvement. In fact, it's not even a book to sit down and read all at once (although if you'd like to, that's lovely). This is a book to

dip in and out of when you feel like you need some inspiration for how to bring a little more magic into your everydays.

You won't find secret hacks to make your life more efficient. We don't offer endless tips for work-life balance or how to "have it all." All that lies within these pages are often overlooked escapes from the busy way of modern day life.

Embrace what you have
We've mindfully created this guidebook so that you don't need a lot of bits and pieces to actually make use of it. Each activity only requires an openness to dream and what you likely already have in your home.

Our approach revolves around appreciating what's in your life already and immersing yourself in idyllic simplicity. You'll see what we mean soon enough and we hope that you love the results as much as we do.

This book is intended for everyone's everydays
Although we've written this book from our perspective, our experiences and our imaginations, our hope is that you find a way to make these stories and activities your own, inspired by your own stories. This book's contents and its offerings are intended for everyone – and is meant to be inclusive to all.

How to start?
Start here and now, by pouring yourself a cup of tea, getting cozy under a soft blanket and slowly exploring the pages that await.

nest

Your home is your sanctuary. It's where you spend most of your time. It's where you unwind, where your family shares their most intimate moments, where you gather and host and celebrate. It is where you rest and recharge and, most importantly, where you grow. Curating your home is something we believe can make your everydays more meaningful. There are endless ways to feel your best when you're there. Welcome back to a space that is yours to discover and fall in love with again and again. **This is your invitation to nest...**

Beautiful Everydays

Home is where she can revert back into her *natural form* – a woman content with solitude and the simplest of pleasures.

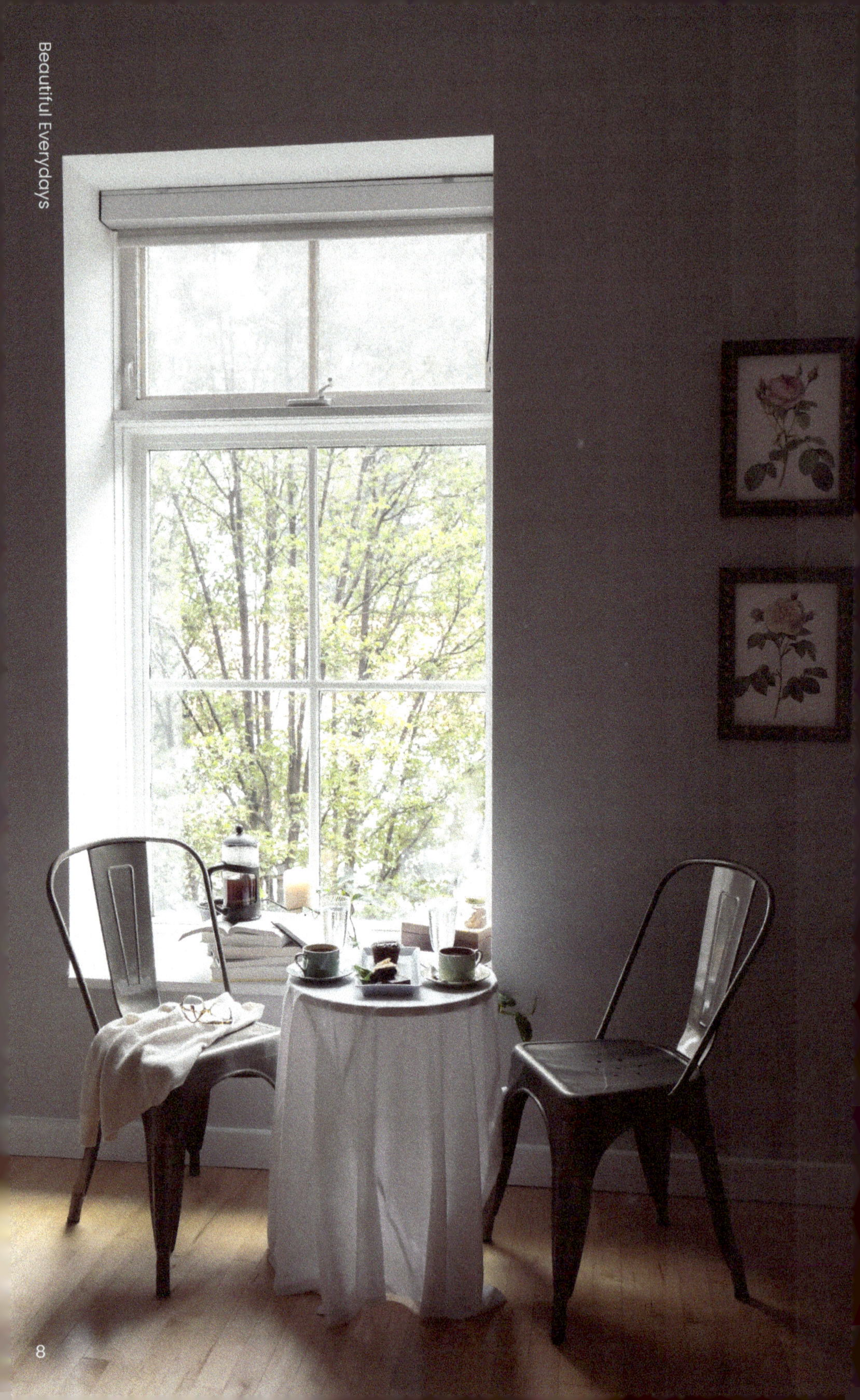

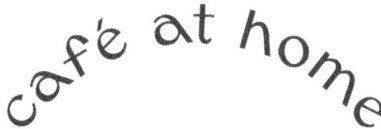

café at home

It was fall in Paris and she sat with her pile of textbooks by a tall bright window. She was supposed to be studying for finals, but was caught up in all the people passing by, each with their own story, their own thoughts, their own plans for the day ahead. Every day, she would choose a new café to visit, sometimes by design, but more often than not by happy accident. Either way she would always order the same thing: a café au lait and a crisp, golden brown croissant. The croissants in Paris were nothing short of divine. Try as she might, she never could uncover their glorious flaky secret for excellence, so she resolved instead to tasting as many as possible during her stay. You know, just to compare of course.

The cafés here weren't like the ones back home. In Paris, even though there were hundreds to choose from, each one had its own *je ne sais quoi;* its own charm, its own personality, its own crowd. She sat for hours, observing the comings and goings about her and then reflected on them in her journal. Sometimes she would get lost in a book; occasionally she would smile at the person beside her or strike up a brief conversation to practice her far-from-perfect French.

Even with a café on every corner, she never tired of each one's unique beauty. She'd step through the doors and immediately feel at ease, comforted by the thought that she could spend some time with herself, in a space she loved.

what's to adore

Whether we're traveling across the ocean or staying put in our hometown, we love frequenting local cafés for a delicious beverage. A frothy cappuccino with foam piled so high it kisses the tip of your nose, a silky smooth latte or an ice cold tea on a hot summer's day; each has its appeal. Add in a sweet treat and a few moments to ourselves for ultimate café bliss.

As we were crafting our morning beverages, we realized there's no reason we can't recreate the same feeling of being at the café right from the comfort of our home.

After all, it's all about the charm and the ambiance. Find a beautiful blend of a few simple elements and you can be transported back to your favourite European spot. All that's required to realize your very own café at home is the imagination to rethink your space.

---

here's how

Find a place in your home
You can create a café in any room you choose – you can even take it outdoors to your balcony or backyard if you have one! Whether it's your kitchen table, your front entrance or even your home office, find a space in your house that can be easily transformed and set up into a café. That means you'll need a table and chair, or at least room for them if they aren't already there. If you can, choose an area by a window so you can replicate that leisurely pastime of watching the world go by, rain or shine.

Set it up
If you're choosing to use your kitchen or office, you probably already have a table, but we like to get creative in using our furniture in unique ways when setting up our café at home. Ideally, find a small side table or round table that's easily movable, along with a chair that fits nicely with it. Place a tablecloth, a picnic blanket or even a crisp clean bed sheet over it and it will instantly make the table feel different, because it's not something you'd typically use with that piece. All of a sudden you have elegant café furniture.

Unpack some ambiance
You know when you go to a café and sometimes they have those charming little flower arrangements on the table? It's simple touches like this that go a long way and there's no reason you can't do the same. Place your own arrangement on the table, or maybe get a few candles from around your house and light them.

Now decide what music you'd like to hear in your café. If it's morning, perhaps you want a happy and upbeat playlist, while for the afternoon you may choose some relaxing acoustic medleys. Is it sunny outside, suggesting a bright playlist? Or is it rainy and calling for something a little more moody? It's your café, so you get to choose what to play!

Another way to create the ideal ambiance is to brew a fresh pot of coffee and place it near your table set-up so you can smell the aroma. If it's a bit chilly, or if your café is set up outdoors, then add a throw blanket or two by your chair for added comfort.

Get fancy, if you like

Now what would any café be without an excellent menu? When it comes to your beverage, it's always nice to have it served in your favourite cup. Maybe that's a fine china teacup or mug that you love. Include any accompaniments that you may need right on the table – a little milk, a small bowl with a few teaspoons of sugar or a teapot under a tea cozy with warm water for refills. And make sure you have treats nearby too! We love a delicious cookie, almond croissant or lemony scone with our coffee or tea. And a little jar of jam on the table just takes it to a new level – trust us!

Froth it up

Frothy milk is like a makeover for coffee or tea and we have a quick and easy way to replicate that café quality foam at home. Warm some milk gently in a pan on your stovetop, stirring regularly, while you wait for your water to boil. Grab a French Press if you have one and pop the warm milk into it. Then, pump the French Press lever up and down quickly for 15-20 seconds and in the blink of an eye you'll have rich, thick foam. Pour the foam into your coffee and gather the rest of the bubbles with a spoon to dollop on top. And voilà! A luxe beverage fit for any seasoned café goer (especially if you add a sprinkling of cinnamon or shaved chocolate flakes on top).

If you don't have a French Press, we recommend still including the warmed milk, because it adds a delicious flavour.

---

accoutrements

- a small table
- a favourite mug or teacup
- some sweet treats
- a simple flower arrangement

make it dreamier

- When we create a café at home, we sometimes like to set the scene by printing a few photographs of the city we're imagining to help us feel what the surroundings might be like if we were truly there. We also love adding in creative objects, art and vintage pieces from around the house that can inspire that vision.

- Why not invite a friend or partner to join you for a coffee or tea date like you would in any other café? You could even try practicing another language with each another. What a lovely way to learn.

- Make your café the place that you reserve for an activity you love. For example, if you want undisturbed reading time, pay a visit to your café. Or maybe you love to knit? Why not block off a regular date with yourself so you can craft the afternoon away.

- Keep that precious coffee hot for as long as possible by warming up your mugs first. Simply pour a touch of boiling hot water into each mug, swirl around for a minute and pour out before filling it back up with your beverage of choice.

don't have what you need?

- If moving furniture feels daunting, choose an area in your home where you can sip your tea or coffee in peace. Maybe this is a favourite armchair, a spot at the dining table or a seat outside.

pairs well with

Escape into Books | Blooming Potential | The Art of Tea

Beautiful Everydays

mood lighting

The bright spark of a match lights her up with delight. Such a minuscule little thing really, daintily poised between her finger and thumb, yet it ignites an instant sort of joy by making the moment feel extravagant, even when it's not.

She's been an inadvertent student of light for a while now. She likes to watch the shadows dance along the walls and tabletops. She likes to gaze at the different shades of light and how each makes everything look slightly different. She likes observing how people are changed by sunlight, firelight, candlelight or lamplight and then keeping those observations quietly to herself.

Embellishing her home with mood lighting helps to break up the day and brings a unique sense of enchantment into better focus, illuminating elements for which she is deeply grateful to experience and that she might otherwise not be able to see.

what's to adore

We design our decor. We design our "life plans" (or at least we brazenly try to). We design our wardrobes and wishlists and dinners and more. Why not put some thought into the light design of our homes as well? After all, light holds a powerful influence over us and can drastically change the atmosphere of a space or event.

In our minds, mood lighting is like creating an artificial sunset or sunrise – a similar feeling takes place that can't quite be described by words alone. We become entranced by how our surroundings transform under different light and we almost transcend into a different mindset.

---

here's how

Dinner by candlelight
The soft flickering of candlelight casts an immediate spell over a space, which is why we highly recommend it for the dinner table. The ambiance wraps around you a little more snugly when candlelight is present. Conversation flows a little easier. Guards are let down and relaxation settles in.

Keep elegant long-stemmed matches (or even regular matches) in a special tin or box and arrange various votives and candlesticks down the center of the table. Afterwards, be sure to enjoy that one-of-a-kind scent that only freshly blown out candles can produce.

Light vignettes
When twilight strikes, turn off the overhead lights in your home and activate alluring little light vignettes instead. These pools of light create splashes of inviting warmth. Table lamps in the front foyer or an otherwise unvisited corner; floor lamps for a pleasant dapple of light in the living room or bedroom; unexpected candle placements on mantlepieces and nightstands. To take all the work out of it, try putting your secondary lamps for these vignettes on timers so every evening, like clockwork, your home is bathed in coziness and the picturesque light design is complete.

Twinkle lights
Twinkle lights – also known as fairy lights – suit just about anything. You can outline floor mirrors with them, run them along bookshelves or window sills, string them up across the ceiling, cluster them together in glass bowls or display

cases... the list goes on and on. Use them as nightlights, decor pieces or for a touch of extra glow in your indoor or outdoor space.

Our favourite way to twinkle light? Save a beautiful empty wine bottle, fill it with twinkle lights and leave it out as a home decor accessory. Part elegance, part imaginative fancy, the twinkle light commands a gorgeous sense of sparkle.

Lanterns

Indoor lanterns are a fun item to bring out when you need a little extra light in your life, because they are so portable. Place them on tables, move them about on the floor, take them outside to your patio or carry them along evening walks. Their animated light is a brilliant and effortless way to bring a homey feeling to the scene.

Embrace the night light
Placing nightlights throughout your home is an instant mood lighting success. From a practical point of view, they make getting up for a late night snack easier (sometimes you absolutely need a cookie in the middle of the night). From a mood point of view, their subtle shimmering is a warm companion for those sleepless nights when you might sit up for a while. Place them in your bathroom, your kitchen, your living room and hallways to make nighttime a little more enchanting.

accoutrements

- candles
- twinkle lights
- lamps

make it dreamier

- While candles are usually most popular at dinner time, they are special anytime. Indulge in some candlelight goodness when you take a soak in the tub, chat with a friend on the phone (or in person) or even while you work – really anytime!

- Activate your mood lighting of choice at a similar time each day so that it becomes a pleasurable routine to look forward to.

- Mood lighting isn't exclusively a nighttime thing. Place a disco ball, big or small, on the floor or on a shelf in the sunniest room in your home and watch dozens of tiny light spots pop all over the space as the sun hits it. Simply beautiful.

pairs well with

Magical Stargazing | Themed Meals | Personal Spa Day

hideaway nook

The snug little corner between her bedside and the wall was her secret hideaway, a place where she could go and be fully undisturbed. A place where her siblings couldn't bother her, where her dreary homework ceased to exist and where she could escape from the chores she had earnestly promised to complete, but didn't want to get around to just quite yet.

Sometimes, after it rained, she could spot a rainbow through the corner of the window, as if it was smiling down on her and her alone. One by one, she would slowly drag her toys into the corner and keep them safe from the likes of show and tell or spontaneous playdates. She had quite the collection of knick-knacks there with no rhyme or reason – but they became her secret treasures.

This little corner housed endless hours of make believe, drawing and dreaming. Calls for dinner would be ignored as she immersed herself into her hidden cove, her happy place, her nook.

what's to adore

When life gets hectic and we feel as though we can't keep up, it's important that we have the tools we need to support ourselves.

It's not always about what you're doing, but where you are doing it. We find value in creating space for ourselves, somewhere that feels like a haven so we can tune out unwanted noise, turn inwards and emerge feeling more centered.

Sometimes all we need is to visit an inviting nook for a break or a bit of rest. Taking time to visit such a place can be very rejuvenating and just the remedy to recalibrate. We believe everyone needs a nook, because it can truly feel like an easy little retreat for the soul.

---

here's how

Define your nook
Whether you're living alone or with others, there has to be a spot in the house that you can retreat to for a few moments a day. Maybe it's by a windowsill, by the foot of your bed, in a wonderfully lumpy armchair or on an outdoor patio swing.

It's a place that you can enjoy and can get some undisturbed time to yourself, where you can close your eyes and let out a sigh because you've arrived. It might be a space that isn't typically used for rest, so use your imagination and look around your home with fresh eyes.

Make it yours
The space you choose may already be decorated or have items scattered about, and that's okay. This isn't about needing to redecorate. It's about utilizing existing items in your home that you find comfort in and gathering them into your nook to make it feel more familiar and personalized. Start by clearing the space of any clutter you don't need or like, so you can start to add more of what you love.

This could vary from a favourite piece of art, to a journal, some framed photographs or some greenery – plants definitely help make a space feel breathable in our experience. And don't forget to add cushions, pillows and blankets into your nook for added coziness.

Envision the vibe
We encourage you to fill your nook with sights and smells that embody your dream vibe. Do darker spaces feel more relaxing to you? Then surround your nook with candles that you can light as you please or put up some curtains that you can draw whenever you want.

Bring in smells that transport you to a state of calm – either through scented candles, incense or essential oils. We love diffusing blends that include lavender and citrus.

And finally, add in some sounds – ocean waves audio, sounds of the forest or music that moves you. Save that playlist as "The Nook" so you can easily come back to it time and time again.

Niche your nook activities
The whole idea of having a nook is dreaming up all of the wonderful things you can use it for! For us, that usually means a combination of the following: reading, meditation, puppy snuggles or writing in a journal.

For you, that might mean painting, stretching, knitting, a nap or even just looking through old photographs. The beauty of a custom nook is that there is no pressure – spend five minutes or an entire hour in it, either way the intention is to help you feel at home within yourself.

Your new tech-free "do not disturb" zone

This part is important. In a world that always feels digitally connected, we're finding that real connection, especially to ourselves, can get lost. We'd like you to dedicate this nook as a tech-free zone... meaning no devices or gadgets (unless it's being used for music).

If you want to take it a step further, create a small sign that you can showcase so your housemates and family begin to honour your time in your nook as well. Rather than the traditional "Do Not Disturb" which feels a bit strict, try "Need My Nook" as a more gentle reminder.

---

accoutrements

- cushions, pillows and throw blankets
- your favourite book, journal or activity
- scented candles

---

make it dreamier

- As with any habit that needs to form, retreating to your nook will require some effort. We recommend developing some sort of ritual to dedicate this time to you. You can either select a specific time that you spend in your nook every day or choose a moment once a week. For example, you could do 15 minutes upon waking or pop in on Friday afternoons. Come up with a symbol to acknowledge the time you'll spend there, such as lighting the same candle upon arrival or ending with a dated journal entry.

- Have kiddos in your life? Come up with a nook for them as well! Kids love to create special spaces they can spend time in – from treehouses, to forts, to indoor tents, it's their way of having a place to call theirs. So why not help them come up with their very own nook that they can visit whenever they want some time to themselves? Sometimes they need a break, too.

no space to call your own?

- If you live in a 500 sq. ft apartment that's filled to the brim (been there), or just have so many people around that you can't find a space to make your own (been there too), we have a secret option for you: make the bathtub your nook once in a while, if you have one. Many people choose to have a tub be their "escape" anyway, so use it to your advantage. Either make taking a bath or shower your ritual, or throw a cushion into your clean and dry tub to create a little haven. The best part, you have a built in "do not disturb" feature with the lock on the door!

- You also have the option of creating a nook outside of your home. Maybe head to a nearby park, surrounded by the beauty and sounds of Mother Nature (just bring along a blanket if you like), or even a café you love.

pairs well with

The Art of Tea | Mood Lighting | Escape into Books

heartfelt decor

Home is her everything. It's the place where she can be with her thoughts, with her ambitions and doubts. It's where she can forsake all pretenses and expectations and revert back into her natural form – a woman content with solitude and the simplest of pleasures offered by the place she lives.

A robust cup of coffee, the feel of an early morning breeze drifting through the windows, some glittering tune dancing in the background and a reliable pair of worn-in slippers. These things are nothing as grand as any mainstream luxury she's told she should want, but she feels very rich with them indeed.

Her home embraces a jumbled assortment of collected memories; bright times from her past, as well as hopeful ideas for her future. From the outside it may not be the most stylish, but she doesn't mind, knowing that her dwelling is meant to be appreciated from within.

what's to adore

We've all heard home is where the heart is, but how much of our heart is actually reflected in our home? Look around you now – how much of what surrounds you is an impulse purchase versus an intentionally placed memory? Decor can be so much more than strategically pulled colours, textures and patterns – it can be personal on every level.

We believe in infusing our homes with as many happy memories as it can hold and then some. We love moving through a room and being reminded of a merry time in our life – be it something from childhood, a trip or a loved one.

After all, life is a journey and we tend to collect mementos of that journey as our everydays unfold, so why not incorporate them into our humble abode? Trends will fade, but a home decorated in heartfelt memories will gracefully grow old with you.

---

here's how

Photos, photos everywhere
If a picture is truly worth a thousand words, why do we typically only display photos in one way – in a frame on the wall or a shelf? Photographs are incredible little time machines that keep a cherished memory alive and they can be enjoyed in unexpected places and ways.

Consider swapping your framed family photos every few months to reflect the mood of the season and rotate your memories. Tuck a few festive photos away with your holiday decorations so that they come out year after year for celebration.

Display travel photos as souvenirs from your latest adventures. And if you don't want them on display, then hide photos in cookbooks and novels so they fall out as a surprise when you pick up those titles again. In short, photographs are always a good idea.

Create a scent story
Every home naturally has a signature scent. But have you ever thought about mindfully creating the scent story of yours? Although not a part of home decor in the traditional sense, we consider it an important part of a home's ambiance. Assign specific candles to the main living areas of your home and burn them

whenever spending time there so the memories become deliciously intertwined with the aroma of the moment.

Keep a bottle of your grandmother's perfume on your dresser and spritz it around from time to time to remember her. Slip bars of scented soap into your drawers – we personally love lavender – to keep things smelling nice and nostalgic. Help your home embody all the happy memories you want to remember by allowing the power of smell to play a part.

Cherish childhood toys

Contrary to popular belief, you don't have to outgrow your childhood toys. We suggest repurposing them into home decor accessories that highlight your style and how you grew up. Stack childhood books horizontally on a shelf so the gorgeous colours on the spine can be enjoyed. Intersperse beautiful stuffed

animals that feel classic and timeless (if they suit your style). Model toys and puzzles can look great on your bookshelves too.

Use toy cars or figurines as paperweights on your desk. Hang artwork from your favourite books or movies. If your parents saved these items throughout the years, then you have countless ways to keep your inner child thriving while making your home decor a little more playful and imaginative.

Frame words that matter

Remember the days of receiving letters in the post or handwritten notes and cards? Where are those items now? Stuffed in a shoebox in your closet or at the bottom of a drawer somewhere? Why not make them a more permanent fixture in your home decor?

Frame those letters from significant others, those greeting cards, those random notes or those scribbled family recipes so their words of wisdom, love and support are always around you. Every time you walk by the frame in question, it will feel like somebody special is speaking to you.

Knick-knacks can be treasures too

The only difference between a knick-knack and a treasure is that one is there unintentionally and the other is wanted. Even the teeniest of items can be a treasure if it means something significant to you.

Perhaps you have a potted plant gifted by your best friend that now rests on your desk and continues to grow along with your goals. Maybe you have an oddball figurine from your first holiday spent with your significant other, before they really knew your tastes.

Did the little one in your life surprise you with a drawing or craft? Did you pick up something on your first solo trip abroad? It's amazing that when you reframe your outlook, anything can be a heartfelt item worthy of being included in your home decor.

---

accoutrements

- letters
- photographs
- childhood toys

make it dreamier

- Consider embracing the idea of handmade home decor elements for a further personalized and sentimental touch. Things like a quilt or blanket, a painted sign, a wooden chest or an accent table will do the trick. Knowing that items in your home were made by the hands of people you love or admire makes the heart swell. Plus, they're one-of-a-kind.

- What to do with all those birthday cards that stack up year after year? Save your favourites and tape them up on the inside of your kitchen cupboard doors. Every time you open them to reach for a plate or a mug, you'll be showered with sweet reminders and notes that you are loved.

not sure where to start?

- Look at the items in your home and try to remember the memory each holds to unlock its sentimental potential. There may be more heartfelt decor moments than you realize already around you.

- If you're feeling overwhelmed by the idea of everything having sentimental value, remember it doesn't have to be everything. Instead choose three things that mean something to you and move them into areas of your home where you can see and appreciate them regularly.

- You can always make a single sentimental statement instead with a piece of furniture that holds a memory. Maybe it's a chair that belonged to your grandmother or a table that once stood in your childhood home.

pairs well with

Keepsake Box | Thoughtful Notes | Mood Lighting

personal spa day

Although she loves a spa experience, she sometimes prefers to slather on a thick clay face mask at home in her favourite pajamas and eat ice cream straight from the container. The idea of pampering herself her way has always been close to her core, even before the term "selfcare" was coined. Back in the day, it looked like sleeping in until noon on the weekends and painting her nails a vibrant red while flipping through her favourite teen magazines.

Now it has evolved into a deeper appreciation for her overall well-being. She honours her mind and body for all it continues to do by moving, meditating and indulging in activities that fill her heart. Once in a while, however, she needs a little something extra – and that's when she converts her bathroom into an at-home spa that only serves the treatments she really loves.

It's usually a fun formula of plush slippers, scented lotions, long showers and a silky bath bursting with bubbles. She spends some leisurely time cocooned in relaxation, sipping herbal tea and poring over magazines like her teen self did, although now they're all about home decor, art and travel. And she emerges feeling like a renewed version of herself. How she wishes she could capture the essence of this day and bottle it up.

what's to adore

Sometimes escaping to a spa when we're stressed isn't possible. Experiencing a balanced life means being able to access a state of calm regularly, not just holding onto our stress and banking it to dissolve whenever the budget allows for it. It's about the little things we can do to recreate that beautiful feeling of bliss, right at home.

One of our favourite ways to do so is through a spa day at home. And if it's not a full day, it's a morning or afternoon, or even an hour. It's about carving out that time to pay attention to you – your most important relationship.

This isn't about forcing yourself to do a 12-step skincare routine (although if that's what you love, then go for it!), but rather it's about creating a ritual for yourself – one that is tailored specifically to you and what you need in order to feel relaxed and worry-free, as often as possible.

---

here's how

Find what calms you
Take 15 minutes and jot down everything spa-like that helps you feel calm. For us, this includes reading a good book, enjoying a hot cup of tea, taking a bubble bath, listening to our favourite playlist, foot soaks, clay masks and moisturizing without being rushed. Think of this as your ultimate calm list that you can refer back to anytime you're craving some rejuvenation.

Create your own spa itinerary
A spa day at home for us can look like this: a light breakfast parfait and a cup of our favourite tea, reading a book while enjoying a foot soak, dry brushing our face and body, applying a body oil and hair mask, taking a long bath or shower (surrounded by candlelight and possibly with a glass of wine nearby) and finishing off with an application of heavenly creams, followed by an afternoon cheese plate! Now it's your turn – what would your spa day include?

Give yourself a hand and foot massage
Of course getting a treatment from a professional is always luxurious, but there's no reason you can't show yourself some love! Our feet carry us all day and we often don't give them the care they need. The same goes for our hands. Take your favourite body oil or lotion and apply generously to your hands and feet. Spend some extra moments on any parts that may feel sore or stiff and give yourself a little massage to help ease tension.

Try a blowout at home
You know what we love? That feeling of freshly washed hair, followed by a mini scalp massage, a few drops of delicious smelling hair products and then a glorious blowout. It leaves you feeling like a celebrity and this is something you can actually try your hand at! It's mainly about setting aside the time to take yourself through each step so the glossy, salon fresh look can be yours after a shower. Sometimes freshly blow-dried hair just gives you that extra boost of confidence for the week ahead.

Dabble with contrast therapy
Start with a warm (or hot) shower, then after a few moments switch to cold water. Alternating back and forth between the two temperatures a few times is said to improve your immune and circulatory system, promote clearer skin and release endorphins. If you've ever done this, you know it definitely feels invigorating. It can even become a part of your daily shower routine.

Practice mindfulness
Whatever your spa day at home involves, one thing that can really help you soak it all in is mindfulness. What this means is simply bringing your full attention and awareness to the present moment.

If we're focusing on an activity, we're more likely to immerse ourselves in it, enjoy the experience and reap the benefits.

For example, if your spa day at home involves a shower, spend a few moments actually noticing the temperature of the water (especially if you're attempting contrast therapy). Pay attention to the way it feels on your skin, to the sound of the water. You can even close your eyes to allow yourself to notice sensations that you may normally tune out.

accoutrements

- your favourite skincare products, bath salts and essential oils
- a glass of wine (or your choice of beverage)
- a good book or magazines

make it dreamier

- It's common to have a large selection of bath products hiding in your cabinets, just waiting to be used. Rather than storing them away, try putting your favourites on display to give yourself more of a spa-like feel. Have some bath salts lying around? Transfer them to a jar to keep by your bathside so you're more inclined to dive in!

- Go retro and get yourself a bunch of magazines. Remember the days when you'd be in a waiting room and your only source of fun was the stack of magazines from six months ago lying on the side table? Somehow they bring such a sense of pleasure and help get our mind off things, even if they aren't up to date. Pair that mood with our comfy robes and we can be content for hours!

- Come up with a signature drink. This is one of our ultimate niceties and you can elevate your spa day at home just by incorporating it! Blend up your favourite smoothie, pour yourself a glass of rosé or create a latte at home.

no time for a spa day at home?

- We're all pressed for time and if the thought of taking an entire day or even an afternoon makes your to-do list automatically grow by three pages, we don't want that. We don't want this to feel like it's adding more stress to your life, so instead we encourage you to choose one or two spa activities to enjoy rather than blocking off a whole day (but the goal is to get there eventually).

- Maybe for now you stick to a smoothie and foot soak, or just 10 minutes for a hot/cold shower, or do a face mask on the weekend. Whatever you decide, try not to rush yourself through it. Savour it, even if it's only for a few moments.

pairs well with

The Art of Tea | Mood Lighting | Blooming Potential

keepsake box

Every now and then her gaze lingers upon the lonesome ornamental box that's been around for as long as she can remember. It's pretty in its own plain way, but also somewhat despondent for it doesn't have, nor has it ever had, any specific purpose.

It's sort of part of the decor, even though nobody really chose it. It's sort of a family heirloom, even though nobody really knows who it used to belong to. It's sort of just... there, empty in every sense of the word. It's not the sort of thing she can simply get rid of either, because it's been a part of her home for so long that to unceremoniously remove it just wouldn't feel right.

Strangely, it's almost a reminder that the small details making up a life can end up forgotten. But today, she picks the vessel up, truly appreciating its presence for perhaps the first time and decides right then and there to claim it as a keepsake in her own way.

what's to adore

Don't we all have at least one random decorative jar or box lurking on a shelf or tucked away in a display case? We either received it as a generic gift once upon a time, picked it up on a whim while out and about or can't quite recall how it came into our possession.

Not typically fans of unsentimental clutter, we find it tricky to justify keeping such an item around. Yet at the same time we don't want to discard it because on some level it appeals to us. Fortunately, there's another option – to fill it up with unabashed joy.

Making a random jar or box into something more pleasant that can be cherished for many years to come is simpler than you might think. All you need is an appreciation for the present and sentimental details.

---

here's how

Make a standing candy dish
There's rarely a time of day when we're not ecstatic by the appearance of a sweet treat in our sights. So it's an obvious solution really – to transform that otherwise impractical bauble into a vibrant candy dish.

Fill it with your favourite goodies and place it where you can easily enjoy a bonbon or two as you pass. A desk, an entryway table or the kitchen counter (to keep pesky hunger away while you cook, of course) are fabulous locations; toffees, mints or chocolates can be fun choices to fill it with!

Catch belly laughs
This twist on the traditional swear jar concept is far more fun. Anytime anything makes you laugh in your everydays – really truly laugh – jot it down on a piece of paper and throw it in the box.

Perhaps your little one's mischief made you giggle, maybe your friend or spouse cracked a joke that had you in tears or your pet did something silly. Maybe something happened that you just had to be there for to really get the humour. Commit the memory to paper and the paper to the box.

Then at the end of the year or on a rainy day, open the box and relive those hysterical moments. You'll be amazed at how much you've forgotten – and as you remember you'll be in stitches all over again.

Save wine corks
If popping some bubbly or enjoying a nice bottle of wine is one of your favourite go-to ways for celebrating, consider keeping the corks. Scoop them up after the last glass is drawn and give them a quick spritz under the tap.

Keep a bold marker or pen by your keepsake box so you can easily inscribe each cork with the date the bottle was relished and the reason it was opened in the first place. Then toss the corks in the box and you have an artsy little decor piece and a beautiful collection of special memories.

Mementos in the making
The curious thing about mementos is that you never really know what will become a cherished gem until time shuffles by. So we recommend collecting the odds and ends that are plucked from the enjoyment of simple pleasures.

Maybe you pocket a drink coaster from a particularly great date or bring back a seashell from a glorious sun-kissed day at the beach. Perhaps a ticket stub from a play or a trinket from afternoon tea with your grandparents makes the cut. Gather those sentimental little bits and bobs and tuck them away into your keepsake box. One day, if you're lucky, the seemingly random assortment of souvenirs will be priceless cheerful reminders of happy days.

Fill with activities
Scribble down all the activities that you've always wanted to try and keep them in your trusty keepsake box. This can be anything from spending a day at the park to trying a new recipe. Then whenever boredom strikes you can fish out an idea and you're good to go! Not sure what activities to include? Anything from this book makes a wonderful addition.

---

accoutrements

- random jar or box
- snippets of paper
- a pen

make it dreamier

∴ Invite friends and family to join in the fun. Take turns filling it with everybody's favourite sweets; catch up on what makes your loved ones laugh; and discover what those closest to you consider a treasure worth saving.

∴ Kick the keepsaking up a notch by making your box a time capsule. Fill it with items from your everydays, then seal it up, pop it back on the shelf and make a pact not to open it for one, two or 10 years!

pairs well with

Heartfelt Decor | Hideaway Nook | Time to Toast

basket of cozy

There was once a time when she loved to be anywhere but home. Plans every night of the week, spontaneous road trips on weekends, traveling at every opportunity. She was a city gal, with a small condo that she used mostly when she was ready for a good night's sleep, only to be up and at it the next day. Over time, however, her late-night adventures were replaced with watching movies on the couch, and waiting in bar lines became evenings in with a few good friends, a bottle of wine and lively charades.

She welcomes this change. Life finally feels like it is slowing down and she is readier than she perhaps knew to catch up with it. Then a funny thing begins to stir her heart: she started falling in love with her home. It became the place where she'd want to spend more time than not. It knew her the best, welcomed her at her worst and was there for her whenever she needed it. Her home became a place of comfort, and she started to tend to it the way that it tended to her all of these years.

what's to adore

It's fair to say that we didn't really learn to appreciate our living space until we got older and began to spend more time in it. That's when we realized we wanted our homes to be soft places to land that reflect us. A big part of that is the feeling of comfort. When you come home, you want to feel welcomed from the moment you walk through your door. You want to kick off your shoes, tie back your hair, wash your face and slip into your comfiest pajamas.

We love that feeling and have taken it a step further by curating a small selection of items that instantly make us feel at ease. That way, whenever we return home after a busy day, or when plans fall through, we are instantly able to slip into a cozy setting.

---

here's how

Gather what comforts you most
We mean all of the items throughout your home that bring you a sense of comfort. This can be anything, of course, but some common ones are blankets and throws, warm fuzzy slippers, silk scrunchies and maybe your favourite robe or knitted cardigan.

It can also be items in your closet that make you nostalgic; maybe an old university hoodie that's been washed one too many times, or your partner's oversized t-shirt. In addition to these cozy items, you can also collect things like a favourite book or journal you love to write in.

Find a beautiful basket
Make yourself a basket filled with these items. We like to call it "a basket of cozy" but it doesn't actually have to be a basket – a crate, bin or even a tote will do. Just a dedicated container for your items. You want it to be something that is inviting and appeals to you. And bonus, it will make a statement in your home decor too.

Make comfort accessible
Now find a suitable place in your home for it; somewhere that it will be deliberately in sight and therefore in mind. Or have multiple baskets of cozy depending on the room (for example, slippers and robes can go in your bedroom, and maybe throws and cozy sweaters are for the living room).

Feel the love

Include items that bring you memories of loved ones. Did your grandmother make you a beautiful quilt, or did your favourite aunt knit you an amazing sweater? Maybe those items can go into your basket so there's some extra comfort when you bring it out.

Sometimes, we like to embellish our coziest items by sewing little fabric tags into them with warm messages, funny thoughts and dates… or even just a simple "from someone" or an inside joke to remind us where it came from. It's a silly detail that brings an extra smile when reached for.

Share the cozy

We believe everyone should have a basket of cozy, because it just makes life much more comfortable. And what better time to start this than when you move into a new home? Immediately you want to feel like you've been there all along and add touches to make it feel like your own. So, we suggest putting together some basics to take over to a friend who's transitioned to a new place. This will make for a thoughtful housewarming gift and will instantly make them feel more at ease in their new space!

---

accoutrements

- blankets
- a comfy cardigan or robe
- slippers

---

make it dreamier

- Do you have a pair of reading socks? Add them to the basket! These are socks reserved especially for those days when you want to dive into a good book and curl up on the couch under a chunky blanket with a cup of tea by your side. If you don't own reading socks, any thick wool pair will do! They are basically just… big socks. Slip these on for some downtime.

- Want to warm things up even more in your basket of cozy? How about adding in a hot water bottle or a heating pad for ultimate comfort.

don't have multiple items?

∴ Rather than a basket full of many things, reserve one signature item for when you want to melt into relaxation mode. Find a place for this item so you know where to go when you're ready to get cozy.

pairs well with

Hideaway Nook | Time to Toast | The Art of Tea

wake up + wind down rituals

- ☐ Wake up to a playlist of nature's sounds instead of a beeping alarm clock.

- ☐ Wake up with a good stretch before getting out of bed.

- ☐ Wake up and focus on something to look forward to in the day ahead.

- ☐ Wake up with a few deep belly breaths.

- ☐ Wake up looking through the window at the glorious sky.

- ☐ Wake up and have a glass of warm water with lemon.

- ☐ Wake up with cuddles from your partner or furbaby.

- ☐ Wake up with a few minutes of walking outdoors for some fresh air.

- ☐ Wake up and spend some time working on a project that brings you so much joy.

- ☐ Wake up with time to journal – about anything on your mind.

- ☐ Wind down with a moment to reflect while you quiet your mind from the day.

- ☐ Wind down with a warm bubble bath or steamy shower.

- ☐ Wind down with no screen time at least an hour before bed.

- ☐ Wind down with a cup of calming tea after dinner.

- ☐ Wind down by reading your favourite book in bed.

- ☐ Wind down with a gentle stretch or a sleep meditation.

- ☐ Wind down with cuddles from your partner or furbaby.

- ☐ Wind down with a few drops of lavender essential oil on your pillow.

- ☐ Wind down by thinking about the best thing that happened during your day.

- ☐ Wind down by watching the sun disappear at sunset.

nourish

Food is the key to many hearts. It's something that brings us together, it can evoke memories and reignite emotions just by smelling something familiar from the kitchen. A toppling piece of birthday cake with lots of icing, a pot of thick soup simmering on the stove or making a meal for someone you love – whatever it may be, food holds a special place in our everydays. So we wanted to share some of our favourite ways to incorporate food (and drink) to make even the smallest moments more special. **This is your invitation to nourish...**

She wants her life to be a canvas, *painted* with one experience after another until it is full.

brunch in bed

She's been looking forward to this all week – a scrumptious Sunday morning. The day already begins at a slower pace. No alarm to turn off, no rushing to get dressed, just lounging in her comfy sheets as the sunlight beams through her window.

It's a rare moment where she can just soak in the luxury of rest, of comfort, of peace. She knows exactly what she wants this morning to be – one filled with her favourite things. After a few minutes of journaling, she lights a few candles, plays some slow jazz and heads to the kitchen to prepare her favourite meal of the week: brunch.

Classic pancakes dripping with syrupy blueberries, a warm cup of aromatic Earl Grey tea and on the side, toast slathered with butter and an over-easy egg – because can you really have the sweet without the savoury?

This wholesome at-home habit comes served with a little secret: she will retreat back to her bedroom to enjoy this brunch in all its glory from the comfort of those soft pillowy sheets, crumbs and all – and there's no stopping her.

what's to adore

Breakfast in bed always brings us back to vacationing at a nice hotel, where the morning stretches out and we don't feel any immediate pressure to start our day.

From start to finish, the entire act of room service is pure indulgence. Browsing the culinary creations from the menu in bed, the anticipation of the knock at the door, the hotel staff rolling the tray into the room, only to reveal a beautiful array of delectable treats ready for your pleasure.

We want you to be able to bring that feeling home and recreate it with our take on brunch in bed. This is for those extra slow mornings where consuming a meal should be done both stylishly and comfortably.

---

here's how

What's on the menu
Half the fun of anything is the pleasure of anticipation, so why not start to daydream about your brunch menu the night before, especially if there is some prep involved. Otherwise, give yourself the freedom to get creative and play in the kitchen the morning of, following whatever craving you woke up with.

We suggest a classic brunch formula – sticking to one main dish and a side to keep things simple. Our favourite combinations? A veggie and cheese omelette, a side of toast and a creamy yogurt parfait, filled with layers of hearty granola, vibrant berries and drizzled honey. If you have more of a sweet tooth, then try whipping up some fluffy pancakes and serving them up with a side of roasted potatoes. This golden brunch formula will not disappoint!

Paris is calling
The French know how to make a splendid breakfast (and we think it's even more enjoyable when consumed in bed). If you're lacking inspiration, stick to a French-themed menu and morning. Croissants, pastries and a fresh baguette with butter and jam will all work wonderfully! Ooh la la indeed!

Serve it in style
Find a flat surface that you can use to display all your goodies. We suggest a large serving board, a tray or even a wooden crate! Anything that will stay in place and prevent your tea from spilling will work great. If you don't have a tray, you can also just pull up a small table at the side of your bed to keep things tidy (throw a tablecloth on top to spruce it up).

Bevvies

Brunch usually calls for a great beverage or two. Make it a treat by bringing out a special tea that you've been saving, or turning your regular coffee into a latte! This is brunch after all. Speaking of which, a fabulous brunch is often accompanied by some bubbles. So if that's your thing, pull out the Champagne flutes and pour yourself a glass, topped with some orange juice for a sweet mimosa.

The company you keep

Brunch in bed is incredible as a party of one. But if you have a partner, why not make it a morning date? While prepping the food, add a little love note to the tray along with some fresh florals to really make them smile. Have kids? Invite them to dine with you. We're sure they'd be thrilled to gobble down some French toast while tucked under your covers!

accoutrements

- a serving tray and linen napkins
- candles and fresh flowers
- Champagne and orange juice

make it dreamier

- Slip into your favourite pajamas the night before and have a robe ready to throw on when you wake to really recreate that fabulous hotel stay feeling. Maybe even put on a hair mask while you're prepping brunch for the ultimate morning of selfcare!

- Spend the entire morning (oh yes, the entire morning!) in bed – we dare you. Once you're done brunch, don't rush to get to the dishes. They can wait. Grab a book off your nightstand and get lost in a really great story for a few hours, or if you're with a romantic plus one, enjoy some quality time together.

not a brunch person?

- Make it easier and enjoy your morning coffee or tea in bed instead, taking as much time as you want. Read a newspaper or magazine, dive into a good book, set up a puzzle on your brunch tray instead of food or simply sit back and listen to your favourite playlist.

pairs well with

Escape into Books | Meaningful Playlist | The Art of Tea

beautiful boards

Some of her favourite memories revolve around informality; last minute plans, unscheduled visits, casual hangouts with nothing prepared in advance. When she was newly married, she thought she could map out her social calendar and create endless lists to ensure no detail was missed when it came to entertaining. And when those nights of formal dinners would come and go, she somehow felt unfulfilled.

After having children, planning for perfection naturally became more difficult. She grew more concerned with napping schedules, diaper changes and play dates, and worried less about preparing three course meals served on fine china that never got used.

With age, came maturity. And not in the way she expected. She thought that she'd eventually discover what it took to be more polished, but surprisingly, the opposite occurred. She learned to embrace, and even love, the dishes in the sink when friends would visit, the crumbs on the table from baking (and devouring) cookies with the kids the night before and the snacks thrown together last minute when her sister or best friend popped in.

Gradually, she discovered her appreciation for things happening on a whim. She realized that sharing food with friends didn't have to mean hours of preparation, only to then miss out on the fun because she was busy trying to be an extraordinary host the entire time. Instead, she fell in love with putting food out to graze on at a moment's notice so she could focus on all of the sharing and laughter – opening her up to what truly mattered most.

what's to adore

The idea of preparing and serving a meal to guests at a dinner party is a lovely sentiment, but let's be honest, we don't always have the time, resources or patience to do it. We often get so caught up in perfecting our guests' dining experience, that we miss out on all the conversations that occur (and isn't that the best part?). So we've fallen in love with another way of enjoying food with friends – over beautiful boards.

We want to keep things simple and fun without compromising on the beauty of it all. This is exactly why we've embraced building beautiful boards of food whenever we have company over, or even when we want an exquisite night to ourselves at home with minimal effort.

Boards and grazing platters are a wonderful way to express your artistry, experiment with different colours and textures of food, while still impressing your guests (and yourself)! And best of all, they are easy to put together.

---

here's how

Pick your surface
You may feel like you need a beautiful slate to create a sensational board, like charcuterie, when all you need is a flat surface. Any shape will do and all sorts of things make a great board – a traditional cutting board, serving slabs, trays or plates that you have at home.

Think of different textures, as they can change the way your board is presented. Wood, marble, ceramic or enamel are all options. Sometimes it's easier to set the food if the board has a lip or edge, although it's not necessary. When there aren't any board options, one idea we love is simply rolling out some craft paper on your kitchen or coffee table to build an epic grazing board directly on top.

A new type of mood board
The most classic and popular board type is charcuterie, which is typically a combination of cured meats, cheeses, olives, nuts, crackers and dips. But there are so many other amazing ideas for boards. You can essentially take any meal idea and transform it into a beautiful board to serve. Simply select something based on your mood.

Some of our favourite ideas include: a taco board – a mixture of hard corn shells, with all of the toppings scattered about (imagine the vibrant colours); a fancy

take on crudités – with tons of seasonal raw veggies and various dips; or a brunch board with a mixture of pastries, sliced baguette, avocado, cheese and fruit. The options are endless so don't be afraid to play around and find what works for you.

Start with the focal point

Every good board has some star ingredients that get all the attention. These are the ones you want to place on your surface first, so that you can build around them. Some examples include: the largest block of cheese, colourful dips or anything with liquid that may require you to put it into another dish (such as olives or pickled veggies and jams).

Start with finding a home for these first – small bowls work really nicely. Next, surround the bowls with whatever item you have the most of in a colour (for charcuterie it might be the bread or crackers, whereas for a crudités board, it may be green veggies). From there you want to fill in gaps with any pops of colour – for example, scatter peppers, tomatoes, meats, etc. Work your way from the inside right out to the edges, and use this as an opportunity to showcase your creativity – there's no wrong way!

Beautify it

Once you have all the main ingredients on your surface, there are lots of ways you can take it to the next level. Adding in florals or fresh herb bouquets really makes the ingredients shine and makes your platter look like edible art. Anything works here, whether it's carnations from your backyard, some white daisies or just sprigs of rosemary tied together with simple twine.

All of these things can be tucked in throughout to complete your masterpiece. Another great option is colourful fruit, cut into unique shapes. If you're assembling a brunch board, grab some mangoes, kiwis or strawberries and slice the fruit to display beautifully on your board.

A night of fun

You can apply the same build-your-own board concept to other fun treats as well. How about a snack board, ideal for movie nights? Just stock up on everyone's favourite sweet and salty snacks – popcorn, chips, candy and chocolate – and assemble however you wish on your beautiful board. You just upgraded movie night!

accoutrements

- a flat surface
- your food ingredients
- fresh herbs or flowers

make it dreamier

- Beautiful boards also make a great gift. Have new neighbours? Stop by with a "welcome to the neighbourhood" board full of some of your favourite local treats. Headed to a party? Bring a small snack board with pretzels, nuts and chips as a surprise for the host. That way they get to enjoy the food and have something to keep afterwards. Just be sure to wrap the board to keep everything in place.

- If you're having friends over and really have no time to put something together, then pick a theme and ask everyone to bring one item to contribute to the board. When they arrive, you can have a little party to make a large board together. It's a fun way to involve your friends and to take any pressure off of getting all the ingredients yourself. Plus it'll be extra special to dig into with everyone being involved from the start!

not a fan of grazing style meals?

- Try out the same idea with a dessert board that you can serve with tea or coffee. Just grab a few pastries and cut them into four (doughnuts, cookies and little cakes work well). Then chop up some chocolate, garnish with a few fresh berries and dessert is served.

pairs well with

Themed Meals | Indoor Herb Garden | Dining Al Fresco

time to toast

She likes the subtle swagger that flitting about her home with a cocktail in hand affords; a cozy blur of daydreams and felicity that reassures her anything is possible. Contentment builds within as she settles happily into her downtime, gently rocking cubes of ice against the rim of her glass.

She's captivated by the subtle sound of it accompanied by bubbles fizzing to their own delightful tune. Her intuition, so often drowned out by the noise of over-scheduling, springs back to the surface, relaxed at last to guide her once again for a brief time.

Of course, it's not really ever been about the libations in their literal form – it's about the ceremony of untangling her inner tension and being free to fantasize, if only for a moment. She smiles to herself at nothing in particular, floating further into her blissful bubble to celebrate and toast to the here and now.

what's to adore

On a sticky humid day it can be fun to look forward to the fresh foam of that first sip of beer, the refreshing kiss of a spritzer, or the splash of soda and lime dancing across your lips.

The gentle chime of glasses jostling against one another, the happy chatter that gurgles and the frothy laughter that flickers around the occasion – a simple concoction as beautifully mixed as the drink before you. Happy hour, to us, is a warm pocket of time to gently let loose.

To relish a favourite beverage for the sheer joy of it is to toast yourself, to celebrate a little moment and push back against the busy nature that inevitably lingers over modern day life. So raise a glass to time that is all yours.

---

here's how

Bring out the special glasses
You know the ones we mean – those sparkling precious cocktail glasses on display in your cupboard. The ones you're too intimidated to use because they are either deemed far too expensive or far too fancy to merit being brought out to enjoy.

Crystal whiskey tumblers, edge flutes with gold trim, classic martini glasses, pot-bellied beer tankards, you name it, we want you to dig them out, dust them off and make them the star of your very own personal happy-hour-at-home-extravaganza. Elegant glassware for even the most basic of cocktails or cold drinks instantly feels more sophisticated.

Dress up your bevvy
Now it's time to fill that oh-so special glass and dress it up! An easy and effective way to do this is with the simple addition of ice. Start by experimenting with different types of ice; after all, keeping your cocktail properly chilled is a must for a beautiful beverage. Ice can be chunky, slender, spherical or cubed and each shape gives the beverage an entirely different feel. Pop edible flowers or herbs into the ice trays to create little glacial works of art.

And what drink would be complete without a pretty garnish like fruit wedges, fresh mint or a sprig of rosemary? Or, truly tuck into whimsical elegance and float edible florals right in the drink, because why not? Garnish is to cocktails what accessories are to fashion – they complete the look.

Take happy hour to your happy place
Let's free happy hour from the proverbial busy patio scene and instead introduce it to your personal happy place on your terms, wherever and whatever that may be. A few of our recommended spots to duck away for a sip? Curling up in a favourite chair, swaying on a swing, soaking in the tub or even climbing into bed to enjoy the sensation of fresh sheets during the day.

Blending the elegance of a high-end cocktail experience with the down-to-earth energy of your everyday home life is a guaranteed formula for creating that magical mood we love to embrace.

Make it active
For a change of pace, why not move your cocktail experience from a sitting position into something more active? Take your margarita for a sassy salsa about the living room, paint a little with an old-fashioned by your side or take a turn around your garden with a martini elegantly in hand. We believe happy hour isn't about only sitting and sipping, but rather about dedicating an occasional hour of your day to doing something that makes you happy (hence the name, after all) in a relaxing manner, whatever "relaxing" means to you. The delicious beverage is simply a tasty bonus.

Give a true toast
The clinking of glasses lovingly bumping into one another might be one of the merriest noises we know. And what better way to accompany a cheers of any nature than with a heartfelt toast! We're not talking about a big rehearsed speech, but rather a few meaningful words to commemorate the little things that can make a moment grand.

We personally love using a toast as a means to practice gratitude. Raise a glass to something you're grateful for, be it great company, to a fulfilling week, to fabulous music, sunsets or anything in between. This seemingly small act can help you take stock of life and marks more of our everydays as special occasions.

---

accoutrements

- cocktail glasses
- a happy place
- garnish

make it dreamier

- ∴ Keep a happy hour journal. Dedicate a notebook to your happy hour antics and record what spiffy cocktail you made, what you did to pass the time and what you raised a glass to. These simple lines per entry will make for a powerful and fun account to reflect on in the future.

- ∴ If you happen to keep a chic bar cart or liquor cabinet, swap those store bought bottles for vintage-inspired decanters. Track some down at a flea market or secondhand shop. They lend an old-world charm to this modern day routine.

not into cocktails?

- ∴ Make a mocktail menu instead. The relaxing component of the experience will still find you, no alcohol required.

- ∴ A glass of water becomes more enjoyable when dressed up too. Add some garnish and creative ice to a pretty glass to make hydration an occasion.

pairs well with

Emotional Painting | Moments with Water | Keepsake Box

pretty plating

Her favourite part of any meal has always been the details. At her grandmother's it was the tablecloth draped across the outdoor patio set. She loved how the lace pattern wrapped around the crisp white edges. Her ears filled with the sounds of plates being collected from cupboards that were much too high for her to reach, while the sight of little hand-drawn lemons on the matching bowls and cups set out for lunch was like a painted portrait of summer.

Her grandmother spent the entire morning preparing the feast, her hands wisely kneading dough, stirring pots and sprinkling spice while a radio chattered in the background. There was a little bit of everything presented for lunch and while the food smelled incredible, what she remembers loving most was how gorgeous it all looked, framed by pretty plates laid out on that intricate tablecloth. The vast array of textures and colours made the lunchtime scene a symphony for the senses – even though it was just another casual weekend.

Her grandmother led by example, teaching her that mealtimes were a way to express one's love through food. Now in her own home, what she sets out on a table often ends up as a layered culinary surprise that easily embraces moments of togetherness, big and small.

what's to adore

Chances are, if we asked you to think of your favourite restaurant, the best chocolate cake you've ever tasted or the most wonderful home-cooked dish of all time, memories would come flooding in; memories imprinted by details such as the decor and the dinnerware. In other words, sometimes it's not only the food itself that makes a meal magical, but also all of the elements that surround it.

Whatever your tastes, and whatever you're craving, we want you to discover how you can easily enhance the simple act of eating by learning to plate food beautifully and create a feast for the eyes.

---

here's how

Satisfy your appetite
Maybe you've finally found the time to flip through your beloved cookbooks for a breakfast recipe, just in time to head to your local farmers' market or grocery store to stock up on everything you need. Or you're nearing the end of a busy day where you didn't have a moment to think about what's for dinner so takeout pizza from the corner place will have to do. Either way, choose something to eat or follow what your body is craving and we'll build from there.

Explore your home
When it comes to plating food, anything is possible! This doesn't require any fancy dishes or fine china (although those are nice). Once again, it's about using what you have in fresh ways. Take a walk through your home and see if there's anything you can use to beautify your dining experience. Things like small dishes, vases, jars, wooden or ceramic trays all make wonderful plating options.*

Keep in mind that not all items are safe for heat/oven/microwave or food use, so be sure to double check before you plate.

Let your creativity shine
Once you've gathered your items, it's time to get creative with how to serve your food. This involves looking at your food differently, almost like you're creating a fun art project. One of our favourite things to do is imagine our food in shapes that differ from their original forms.

For example, ordered a pizza? Cut it into little pieces and serve it on a dark stoneware surface, like bite-sized bruschettas! Having Mexican for dinner? Use a combination of smaller bowls to serve your guacamole, salsas and taco toppings.

Plating for kids
Can't get the kids to eat their dinner? A lot of parents can relate to this one! Making food fun for kids increases your chances of the food landing in their bellies rather than the floor. Try using different colours, shapes and textures in the presentation of the food. Maybe cut their grilled cheese into little triangles, stacked on top of a small cup filled with ketchup. Or perhaps alternate layers of pasta and sauce in a clear cup, making a fun striped project that they have to mix up when they eat!

Repurpose your kitchenware
Often we reach for the obvious options when plating food. Salad tongs to serve a salad, soup bowls for soup and wine glasses for wine. But what if we switched it up? Gather your existing kitchenware and look for unique and creative ways to use it.

Try serving side salads with chopsticks instead of forks. Maybe serve your soup in mugs instead of bowls (and save on the utensil washing time), or how about pouring drinks into cozy little mason jars rather than the glasses they typically require? All of a sudden you'll have a number of uses for kitchen items that would otherwise stay hidden in the back of your drawers.

accoutrements

- assortment of dishes and serving surfaces
- additional fun things (linen napkins, napkin rings, whatever you desire!)
- random household items

make it dreamier

- Get creative with your day-to-day meals, not just dinner. Serve up a simple sandwich lunch on a small wooden serving platter with a side of chips, or build your morning parfait in a wine glass so you can see and appreciate all of the layers, colours and textures.

- Try serving water in a pitcher with slices of cucumber, lemons and oranges for some added beauty. Not only will this be fun to drink, but it doubles as a colourful centerpiece for your table too.

don't feel like going all out?

- Do the same with aperitivo. Simply get creative with the way that you're plating your snacks. Try a mixture of nuts, seeds, dried fruits and some chips and display them using a collection of tiny dishes.

- If you feel your serveware is lacking presentation, check out local secondhand options for some inexpensive repurposed goods that you can pick up. Or host an exchange with your friends or neighbourhood – you might find some gorgeous hidden treasures!

pairs well with

Dining Al Fresco | Brunch in Bed | Beautiful Boards

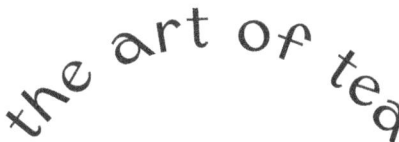

the art of tea

The familiar pace before a busy day begins as soon as she climbs out of bed – she brushes her teeth, showers, does her skincare regimen, gets dressed. But the last beat of her morning routine is what she looks forward to the most – the slow ritual of switching on the kettle and waiting for the water to warm.

She takes a deep breath and ponders which tea will suit her best today. The sky looks grey and she can hear raindrops softly pattering against the window, making it just the right occasion for a cup of traditional English Breakfast. It's here that she'll stay for as long as time will allow, in the simplicity of steeping and sipping.

She revels in the calm before the fullness of her day seeps in. To-do lists are forgotten, problems are put on hold and she basks in this glorious moment that has become a welcome reprieve in her everydays where she feels still and peaceful. It's just her and her cup of tea for the next few minutes – and it's glorious.

what's to adore

A cup of tea can mean so much. It's an extension of warmth to create a connection with a stranger, to catch up with a neighbour, or to be there for a friend in need. Sometimes, it's a way to signal a start to the day; other times, it's a much needed afternoon break that pairs nicely with a sweet treat! It also calms our nerves and soothes our racing minds after a difficult day to help us get a better night's sleep.

For us, tea almost always offers a welcome pause. It creates a moment to enjoy, even in the most chaotic settings. The art of tea is one of life's simplest pleasures, bringing the gift of stillness so you can enjoy the present.

---

here's how

Create a tea station
Whether it's a cabinet or an area on your kitchen counter, create a little tea station where you can keep your kettle, teapot and selection of teas so you can find exactly what you want, when you want. Then arrange your tea station in an inviting way. Maybe you store your teas in a tea chest or in an old biscuit tin – display it in a way that brings you joy every time you make a cup.

Select a tea to suit your mood
Different teas can soothe us in different ways. Choosing a tea intentionally can help provide relief for whatever feelings might be present. Here are some suggestions on selection:

- Classic English Breakfast or Chai to help kickstart your day
- Peppermint to sip after lunch for a refreshing afternoon
- Chamomile before bed to calm you (or mint again if you prefer)
- Weekend tea: Cream of Earl Grey served alongside pancakes

Picking your cup
Cups and mugs are all about personal preference – choose an oversized mug that makes you feel like you're on a camping adventure in the great outdoors, or select a dainty cup that reminds you of having a tea party. Perhaps there is a mug brought back from an incredible vacation as a souvenir, or one that is slightly chipped but was passed down to you from your grandmother. Choose thoughtfully to enhance the experience.

Steeping

This is the perfect time for a mindful moment – place the tea bag or leaves in your cup, and now pay close attention… for loose leaf teas, do the leaves change shape? Are the dried petals uncurling slowly, as they get enveloped in the boiling water? What about a tea bag – notice the water changing colour as the flavour slowly seeps out. The process is slow and artful, if you pause to notice and appreciate it.

A spot to sip

Do a check-in on how you feel and what you need from your tea time. Depending on that, you can then decide where you want to enjoy it. Need to unwind? Sit by the window and have a look outside. Feeling down? Head to your favourite spot on the couch and curl up under a blanket. Need some socialization? Invite a friend over for tea and enjoy it in an outdoor setting. Something to celebrate? Put the kettle on and take yourself for a twirl around the kitchen.

Sipping slowly

The beauty of tea is that it cannot be experienced quickly. Even if slowing down doesn't come naturally to you, tea requires time and we have to wait patiently for it to steep and cool before we can take our first sip.

Use this as a little extra mindfulness moment – close your eyes and breathe in the aroma of your tea, let out a deep breath to cool it and enjoy the feel of warmth that the cup provides. Once you start sipping, savour the flavours.

accoutrements

- selection of your favourite teas
- kettle and steeper (if you're using loose leaf tea)
- a favourite mug or cup

make it dreamier

- Tea is a wonderful excuse to enjoy your favourite dessert (not that we personally need an excuse). Here are some of our top pairings: lavender shortbread, scones with jam, classic chocolate chip cookies or a slice of carrot cake with rich cream cheese icing.

∴ Gather a group of friends and host an afternoon tea party – for an occasion or for a simple catch up. You can even mail invites, ask friends to dress up and pull out your favourite serveware. It doesn't take much effort to put together a few savoury and sweet options – some finger sandwiches, sweet treats and little chocolates will do the trick! An easy way to make a regular Sunday afternoon (or any afternoon for that matter!) a special one.

not a tea person?

∴ You can still take a much needed moment to yourself with any warm beverage. A cup of coffee is usually a favourite alternative, but we also like switching it up with a mug of hot chocolate (especially during colder months – whipped cream or marshmallow toppings and all), apple cider or even a glass of hot water with some freshly squeezed lemon.

pairs well with

Pretty Plating | Café at Home | Ode to Cookies

Nourish

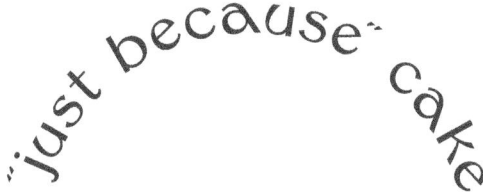

"just because" cake

She was at her best friend's house, watching her blow out the eight bright flickering candles on her birthday cake. She couldn't keep her eyes off of it. "Hurry up already!" she thought to herself. Yes, of course she cared about her friend turning another year older, and about the games they were going to play and the goodie bags they would get to take home at the end of the party. But what she couldn't stop thinking about was that cake. That wonderfully layered, delicious, pink and white icing covered cake!

She teetered on her tip-toes, peering over everyone in an effort to catch a glimpse of the first slice. Ohh! Chocolate AND vanilla on the inside! And there were sprinkles, lots of sprinkles. She really hoped she would get the slice with the purple flower and a little bit of the "H" from the icing. Score! She was handed her piece and sat eagerly, gobbling the sweet, buttery cream decadence and for a few moments, life had never been better.

All these years later, every time she sees a birthday cake her eyes light up and she can remember that exact taste. Cake transports her to moments of celebration, of her youth and playfulness, to a time where the only thing that mattered in the world was getting the biggest piece.

what's to adore

What's not to love about cake? Luckily cake is something that we never outgrow. In fact, the more grown up the special occasion, the more elaborate the cake becomes. Birthdays, bridal showers, anniversaries, baby showers, weddings, retirement parties and more! Not to mention the flavours… they just get more sophisticated and imaginative over the years.

But what about all those other moments that are wrapped up in your everydays? The ordinary occasions that are just as meaningful, but not as welcome in mainstream party circles. Occasions like making it to the end of a tough week, or checking something off your to-do list?

We believe that cake doesn't need a special occasion to exist. And the best part of a "Just Because" cake, is that you get to make it whatever you want, however you want and whenever you want.

---

here's how

Pick a flavour
Craving something light but decadent? Maybe it's classic vanilla with sprinkles and white icing, or double chocolate with chocolate icing for good measure. Want to try something more elevated. We love strawberry cheesecake or coffee cake. Obsessed with cream cheese icing? Go for a carrot cake or red velvet. Feeling extra indulgent? How about a flourless chocolate cake with a molten center? There is no shortage of cake flavours, all you have to do is choose one.

Immerse yourself in the baking
You might be someone who bakes often, or maybe you've never made a cake before. Have you ever done an activity where you're completely in the zone and focused with full involvement and enjoyment in the process of what you're doing? This is what we want you to feel when you're baking.

Cake making is the most fun when we stop worrying about the clean up (especially if there is flour flying around everywhere and spills on the counter), the dishes and whether or not the cake will rise to perfection in the oven.

Lick the spoon, try cracking those eggs with just one hand, whisk away until your heart's content and maybe even sneak in a few bites of icing in between. The kitchen is your playground and there are no rules, so go wild!

Embrace the imperfection

This part is really important. It may even be the secret ingredient to a "Just Because" cake. As adults we often put a ton of pressure on ourselves to make things perfect. It's usually the reason we don't attempt things in the first place, because we're scared the end result won't match our expectations. Well this is the point where we say throw those expectations out the window.

Did your cake crumble when you removed it from the pan? Oh well. Gather those pieces into a bowl, pile on a big dollop of icing, grab some forks and call it a day. Want to slather each bite with icing? Maybe scoop some ice cream on top? Great! There is no right way to do this, so don't be so hard on yourself.

Decorating, your way

Decorating your cake doesn't mean you have to attend a professional cake class to learn the art of fondant. Naked cakes are just as beautiful and don't require much fussing. If you do want to add some embellishments, experiment with toppings like crushed nuts, chocolate shavings or shredded coconut.

If you want to beautify it further, try adding some florals on top (simple baby's breath looks lovely, as well as pops of bright blooms*) or fresh fruit, like thinly sliced strawberries. Remember, you're going for messy decadence here.

Keep in mind that not all flowers are edible.

---

accoutrements

- apron
- icing and sprinkles
- your sweet tooth

---

make it dreamier

- Baking a cake for yourself is such an act of self-love, but if you feel like passing some of that on then bake a cake for someone else! There's always something to celebrate, so why not do so with this thoughtful gesture?

- Place your "Just Because" cake on a cake stand. It's like a little pedestal on your kitchen counter, serving as a friendly reminder that you are free to celebrate anything, big or small, simply because you want to.

what if I can't bake?

- If you've tried a bunch of times and just can't get into baking or don't enjoy the process, that's more than alright! You can still have your dessert and eat it too. We suggest picking up a cake from a favourite neighbourhood bakery or better yet, head to a grocery store and grab one of those sugary slab cakes (that'll definitely take you back to grade two).

- You can still decorate a store-bought option at home to make it extra special. Or just dig in as is – we won't judge.

pairs well with

Blooming Potential | The Art of Tea | Café at Home

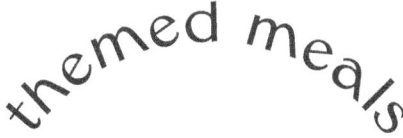

themed meals

No matter how many planes she gets on or how many places she visits, she never fails to be astounded by the creativity of food – and the rich cultures that surround it. With each new stamp in her passport comes a collection of unforgettable experiences, many in which food takes the center stage.

There was that summer in Italy – drinking wine in the local piazza with friends, trying double espressos and living off pasta, pizza and gelato because when in Rome, right? Then there was Mexico for a post-grad trip complete with late night dancing, frozen margaritas and the best tacos of her life. And how could she ever forget Morocco, where she discovered fresh oven-baked flatbreads that soaked up an array of flavourful creamy dips.

She considers herself an explorer and a wanderluster, who is constantly curious about the world and its many flavours. Each time she's away from home she returns with a fresh passion for cooking and more recipes than she could ever make in her lifetime.

what's to adore

When we think about exploring food as an experience, our minds go to the idea of travel and the privilege of partaking in a destination's restaurants and many culinary traditions. It's easy to believe that the only way to get creative with food is to get away or dine out, but our home kitchens are brimming with magic.

A great way to tap into a creative food experience is to build themed meals at home that transport us to another place, another time or a happy memory. By honouring the nuance of flavours and the rich stories that so often accompany food in general, themed meals are a wonderfully fun way to learn and connect.

Whether creating a themed meal through an educational lens, a personal lived experience or a passion for fictional escape, so many places and times can be reached without leaving your home.

---

here's how

Pick your theme
With so many incredible theme ideas to choose from, it can be hard to pick just one. Start by making a list of a few places that you wish you could visit or revisit, or an era that you've always wanted to experience. Select the one that stands out most to you right now. Craving a beach getaway? Go with a Jamaican or Balinese theme! Wish you could get lost meandering narrow cobbled streets? Then take yourself to the streets of Lisbon with a Portuguese themed dinner. How about a roaring 1920s themed dinner party? Or imagine a futuristic food theme for fun? The possibilities are endless.

Plan the menu
Open yourself up to the excitement of learning all about new cuisines and flavours from others. Spend some time researching popular dishes for the theme you have in mind – focus on a wide spread of apps, mains, dessert and even drinks.

For example, if you've chosen Thailand as a destination, learn about the different ingredients used to make some of their popular dishes. We're thinking lemongrass, sweet basil, red chillies, mangoes and coconut milk. You may also be able to find a market or shops nearby that carry international ingredients. And don't forget about a refreshing beverage, like Thai iced tea or a popular Thai beer or whiskey.

And if cooking isn't your thing, remember you can always order in! Find an authentic restaurant near you that specializes in the cuisine you'd like to experience, and dinner is served.

Include details
Now that you've covered taste, think about the sites, sounds and smells of the theme you have chosen. Find decor to match! Maybe it's hosting a meal inspired by your favourite book or film. Try to be as true to the theme as you can to create the look you're going for (think lanterns/lights, fabrics, dishware, etc.).

In terms of sounds, what is the music like? Find a playlist with musicians and songs that reflect your theme. Or create a soundtrack that matches the surroundings.

A reason to gather
Since you're cooking, why not invite friends along to join you? It'll be like you're vacationing or time traveling together for the night! An easy way to do this without feeling overwhelmed is to turn the gathering into a potluck.

Each person can select a dish or drink to bring from the theme you've chosen. That way you'll have ample amounts of food without the pressure of having to make it all yourself. Or host a cooking party so you can chatter, cook and explore in the kitchen together.

Go deeper

Help your guests feel connected to the theme by creating a trivia game around it that brings to light fun facts and history about the theme you've chosen. That way, it's an opportunity to combine learning with the experience. And maybe the winner gets first dibs on dessert?

accoutrements

- cloth napkins
- playlist
- serveware

make it dreamier

- Rather than dinner, pick a different time of day to host your meal. Maybe you prefer brunch – there are so many incredible options that offer a unique take on brunch. Maybe you go 80s diner style, or recreate a theme from a show you watched as a kid on Saturday mornings.

don't want to focus on one theme?

- If the idea of building a meal around a specific theme feels too much, simplify it instead. Keep the potluck concept and make your theme "everybody's favourites." For example, you could build it around their favourite casserole recipe of all time, their favourite childhood meal, their favourite comfort food, sweet treat or favourite seasonal dish. Playing up favourites opens up a whole range of theme options that are easy and fun to pull together.

pairs well with

Mood Lighting | Dining Al Fresco | Pretty Plating

an ode to cookies

- ☐ Cookies go with coffee or tea in bed – and are especially divine when dunked.

- ☐ Cookies accompany late night calls to your bestie living on the other side of the world.

- ☐ Cookies are good company on random strolls to the water while staring at the horizon.

- ☐ Cookies can be shared with strangers on the bus stuck in traffic.

- ☐ Cookies help reveal to a secret crush that you're into them.

- ☐ Cookies slip easily into a purse for emergency snacking.

- ☐ Cookies break the ice with new friends and fill the silence with old ones.

- ☐ Cookies should be mandatory at all meetings.

- ☐ Cookies are a peace offering.

- ☐ Cookies belong at tea parties – real and imaginary alike.

- ☐ Cookies can be eaten anytime at all – no need to tell anyone.

- ☐ Cookies make happy occasions happier and sad ones a little more bearable.

- ☐ Cookies straight out of the oven are a risky business (and totally worth it).

- ☐ Cookies inspire delightful words like "ooey gooey" and "scrumptious."

- ☐ Cookies ought to be eaten two at a time on lazy Sundays spent at home.

- ☐ Why make lemonade when you could make cookies?

- ☐ Don't cry over spilled milk – soak it up with cookies.

- ☐ We can still be friends if you don't like cookies – we'll eat yours.

- ☐ Saving the last cookie for somebody else is true love.

- ☐ Cookies taste best outside.

- ☐ Cookies taste best inside too... (we've checked!)

- ☐ Cookies pair with scribbling in notebooks, even if your hands are covered in ink.

Beautiful Everydays

nurture

One day we're playing in a sandbox, covered in dirt with a giant smile on our face, the next, we're the ones asking kids to put that same dirt down. What happened between those innocent fun-filled years and now, where life is about planning and scheduling and rules, leaving very little room for much else? We're talking about play. About the ability to find joy in the smallest things, like we did when we were little. Where we would run wild and free and be completely present and immersed in whatever activity we were doing because we didn't know any other way. It's time to get reacquanited with your inner child, and bring some wonder back into your everydays. **This is your invitation to nurture...**

Beautiful Everydays

She disappears into a world of words not because she wants to *escape* from life, but because she wants to explore as much of it as she can.

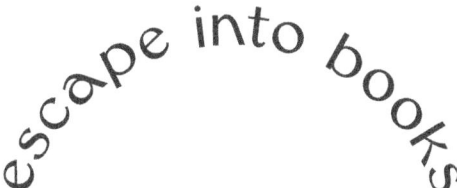

Although enchanted by the unassuming magic of time at home, her wild imagination and natural curiosity cannot be contained. And when the call for adventure beckons, there's only one way to satisfy an insatiable lust for new wonders and fascinations – her beloved books.

Each turn of a page transforms longing into a riveting experience. The intoxicating aroma of crisp paper and ink unfurls into a slow afternoon or the early hours of a quiet morning. Daydreams feel alive and possibility is placed within reach.

She disappears into a world of words not because she wants to escape from life, but because she wants to explore as much of it as she can. She journeys inward, delving into thoughts, feelings, characters and stories while absorbing the lessons within what is written, and allowing space for such things to imprint upon her heart.

what's to adore

It's ironic that when it comes to trying to describe our deep love of books, we can't quite find the words. We fall head over heels in love with characters, plots and new worlds time and time again, like we did when we were little and camped out under the covers with a flashlight or hid away in the treehouse with our favourite adventures.

Reading makes your heart want to burst. It transports you to places you might otherwise never see, it introduces you to people you might otherwise never meet and it teaches you lessons that you can't even begin to dream. There's not much we can recommend to make books better, but we do have a few tricks up our sleeves to help you fall even more deeply in love with them.

---

here's how

Set the scene
When it comes to devouring a story of any kind, ambiance is half the flavour, so choose your reading locale wisely. Wading through a salacious thriller? Bundle up under blankets in bed for added safety. Launching into a fantastical adventure? Camp out under a majestic tree in your nearest green space. Skimming a decadent cookbook? Perch yourself in an elegant dinette.

The theme between book and setting doesn't have to be symbiotic, but being mindful about where you crack your next cover can infuse your literary experience with a whole new level of enjoyment. It's as though you become a part of the text. And remember, the most ordinary spaces can sometimes hold the most imaginative potential.

Dress it up
It's customary to have a go-to outfit for date nights, for pool parties and hitting the gym, so why not make dressing up for some quality time with your current novel a custom too? Our advice? Dress up… comfortably! If that means adorning a favourite scrappy sweatshirt – go for it! If that means a flowing robe – make it happen. A stretched out sweater with no shape to it at all – absolutely fantastic. Just ensure that whatever your go-to reading attire is that you feel relaxed and are able to curl up in it for added comfort.

Choose a scent
Intentionally choosing a scent – be it a candle or an aromatic diffuser – for our reading habit adds an exquisite layer of sentimentality to the story at hand.

When rereading a favourite book, revisit the scent you designated for it and it'll bring you back to that indescribable first time you discovered the story at hand.

Leave yourself a note
Slip a piece of paper inside the front cover with a note to self. Jot down the date when you last finished reading, how the book made you feel and what you learned from it. If you ever reread the book, future you will love discovering what younger you thought. If you pass the book on, somebody else will get to see your insights.

Mix it up
As much as a reading routine helps us dedicate regular time for our bookish dalliances, it's important to keep in mind that a routine can be flexible. In other words, we don't always have to reserve the hour before bed for story time.

Try mixing up your reading time for an entirely different mood; get up at the crack of dawn and read while the birds start to stir, sneak away at noon and bask in the sun as you soak up a new text, or reconnect with your inner child and stay up until well past midnight with the page aglow by the lamp on your nightstand. Embrace the time of day that feels most magical for you.

---

accoutrements

- cozy feel-good clothes
- your read of choice
- scented candle or diffuser

make it dreamier

∴   Use a favourite printed photograph as a bookmark. This way, every time you flip back to your page, you come face-to-face with a memory that makes you smile.

∴   Novel nibbles are a delight! Our appetite for poetic prose is only rivaled by our never-ending love of snacks, so it's not a surprise that we advise working a gratifying morsel into your reading routine. Sweet or savoury, keeping something in the pantry especially for book time makes you look forward to diving into the next chapter even more than that cliffhanger.

∴   For those literary lovers, pick up a pen and scribble (yes, scribble!) right into your book. Underline passages that move you, circle phrases that take your breath away, write thoughts and reactions in the margins. All the literary greats do – you can too!

not a big bookworm?

∴   All of these recommendations can be used to embellish flipping through a magazine, spending time with a sketchbook or jotting things down in a notebook.

∴   Bring back the tradition of storytelling. Gather a group of friends or family and take turns reading parts of the book aloud to each other. Get into the characters as much as you can!

pairs well with

Basket of Cozy | "Anywhere" Picnic | Ode to Cookies

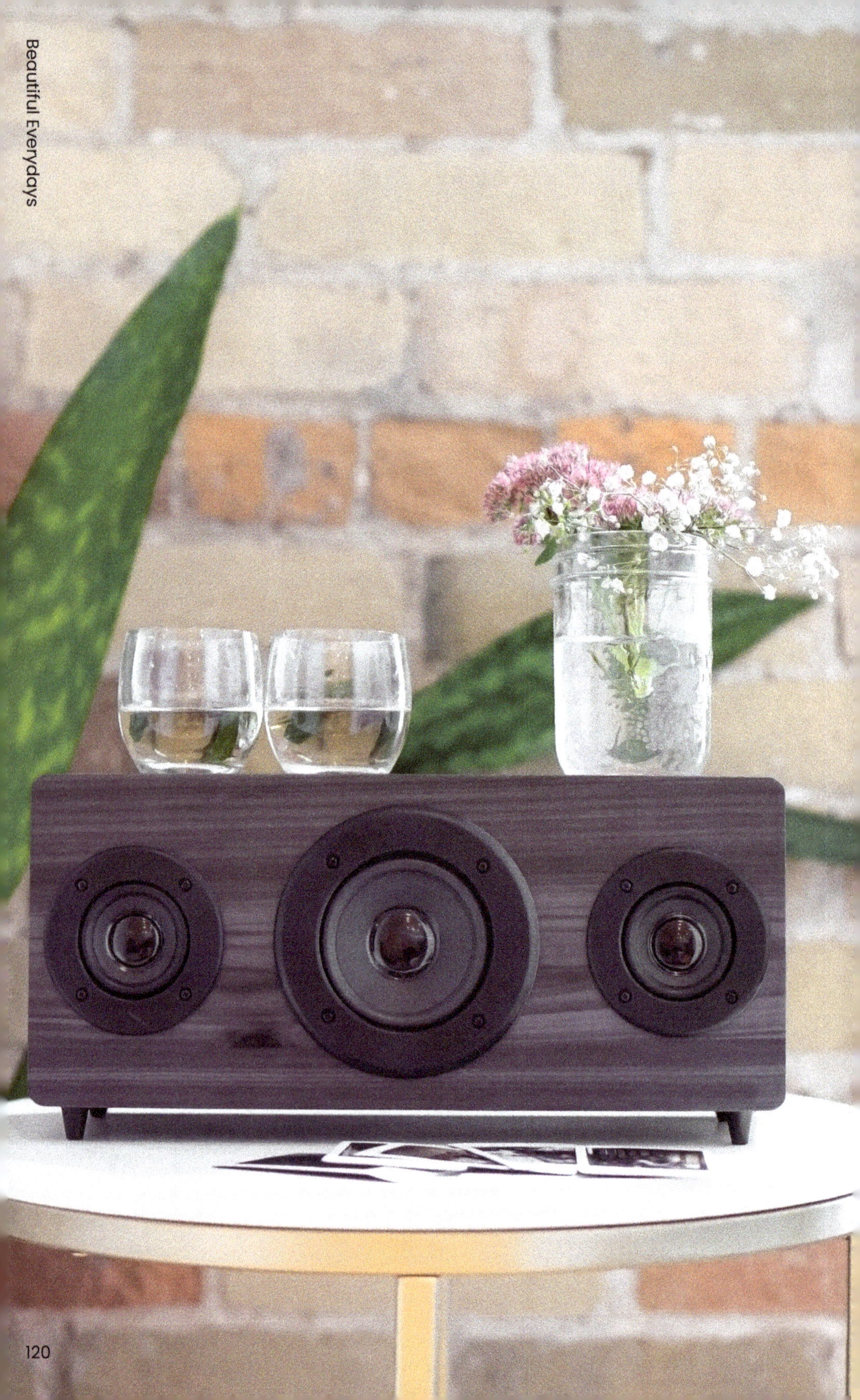

meaningful playlist

Her mother used to tuck her in at night, press play on a cassette and leave the door open just a sliver to make nighttime more inviting. The tune would inevitably vary; sometimes it was the same tape played on repeat for weeks on end, other times it was changed every evening for an exciting new band, but it was always a comfort that whisked her off to sweet dreams.

It's a habit she's carried with her ever since. Whenever fear or uneasiness of the unknown overcomes her, she slips back into the world of music to soften and refresh her energy. Over the years she's noticed she listens to song lyrics more and more, compelled by their poetry and ability to express intangible emotions.

When she can't articulate her thoughts or overactive imaginings, music is there to say everything she can't – and more. And for all the other times, it's simply good fun.

what's to adore

It's common knowledge that song inspires dance and dance inspires joy. But the modern day way of consuming music has dulled some of its fabulousness in our opinion. We often put it on in the background instead of making music the main event.

One way to reclaim the magic of music is to curate your own playlists from the heart. Don't just accept what somebody else is broadcasting – dig into the rich musical library of your life and pull out songs that make you feel alive.

The trick to building a meaningful playlist is to load it up with songs that resonate with your unique experiences – melodies and lyrics that sweep you away into the recesses of happy days gone by. Reflecting upon past events is a terrific way to mine your soul for the soundtrack of your life. And then, we recommend cranking up the volume.

---

here's how

Summer anthems
Think back to your favourite summer of all time – was it the year you spent every weekend swimming in a lake? Was it the year you stayed out late night after night at the drive-in with friends? Or that steamy summer when you stole your first kiss and left weekly love notes in their mailbox? Every summer naturally has an anthem, a song that when you hear it carries you back to the humidity and warm breezes of those endless outdoor infused days.

Tunes that remind you of your family
All families have their own music history. There's the tune that pops up from time to time and elicits, "Oh this is MY song!" from your parents. There's the golden oldie that your grandfather says got him through some rough times. There's the music that is blasted at family get-togethers or a rockstar's greatest hits that you all soaked up at a concert together. Your family's musical memories deserve a track on your playlist. So load up any medleys that remind you of your nearest and dearest.

Pull songs from your big events
Was there a song that everybody went bananas for at your wedding or birthday shindig? A song that brought people rushing to the dance floor? Was there a specific album you found yourself listening to on repeat during a solo trip abroad as you explored new cities and spaces? Add it to the list! Was there a

song from your junior prom that you remember your secret crush asking you to dance to or that you and your friends went wild for? Populate your playlist with big memorable event tunes.

Curate music to mood
Sometimes we need a good cry – we just do. Create an arrangement of songs that pull on your heartstrings to inspire a flow of tears and release. It sounds like a somber playlist might be sad, but sometimes a good cry can be refreshing.

Or you might want a dreamy romantic feeling, so put songs together that remind you of the time you belted out terrible karaoke with your partner or the intimate dinner date you had in that little place that nobody remembers the name of. Whatever the tone you want to strike, a thoughtfully put together playlist works wonders to accentuate the mood of a moment.

Really listen

Spend time truly listening to your playlist. Don't just throw it on in the background while you're busy doing something else; make it the main focus. Find a favourite spot to sit or sprawl for a while and hit play. Soak up every beat, every instrument, every sound and rhythm and focus wholly on the notes that are dancing within your ears. It's amazing what you can hear when you really stop to listen and drink it in.

accoutrements

- your speaker of choice
- your wildest dance moves
- a little nostalgia

make it dreamier

- You can have many, many sentimental playlists. Curate a different one for all sorts of occasions and pair them with activities beyond working out. For example, perhaps you have a gentle playlist for mornings spent creative writing. And another for when you have friends over for drinks. Date night with your better half? Throw on a playlist that is filled with memories shared by just the two of you.

- It might be hard to create an entire playlist on vinyl, but embracing a vinyl album for the rich crackly pops and distressed sound can be extremely powerful and beautiful. See if you have a favourite retro album that you're in love with and bring it out for special listening.

pairs well with

Café at Home | Emotional Painting | Hideaway Nook

playtime with pup

As sunlight creeps across the floorboards, a tail gently wags with quiet satisfaction. Its movement raises a tiny cloud of dust that twinkles in the golden light as lanky legs stretch and sprawl, greedily soaking up the final warmth of the day.

Her truest of friends, her most faithful and loyal companion – her darling pup, who has been with her through all the ups and downs of perpetually growing up. Nobody sees her quite like those sweet soulful eyes. Nobody stands by her side quite like that steadfast barrel-chested presence. Nobody greets her as excitedly as that giant slobbery grin brimming with enthusiasm.

Love runs throughout her life carried by these four clumsy paws. Whether nestled together on the couch or frolicking in the great outdoors, this is a duo joined by the soul.

what's to adore

Have you ever come home after a horrible day and been greeted at the door by your dearest dog and their carefree quirks? Has your heart ever skipped a beat when a dog seemingly vibrates off the ground with exhilaration just because you said hello or looked in their general direction?

In our books, dogs are magic. Pure and utter magic. They are a constant source of comfort, loyal protectors, jolly entertainers and endless bundles of love. Sprinkling everydays with extra quality time for the dogs in our lives is a way to deeply connect with one of the simplest and most profound joys of this world – darling, delightful camaraderie that has no comparison.

---

here's how

Make laundry a game
Fresh or filthy, it doesn't matter when it comes to making laundry your pup's new favourite shenanigan. They will likely revel in the energetic escapade and you get to spruce up an otherwise tedious chore. Simply toss your laundry into an inviting messy pile (on the floor if needing to be washed; on the bed if freshly laundered) and start tussling with your dog between sorting, folding and hanging! Soak up the bounces, the hyper energy and the hilarious glee.

Explore a new walk
Breaking out of your usual routes transforms the daily walk from "something that has to be done" into an opportunity for glorious adventure. Take a turn about your neighbourhood using streets you don't normally frequent or visit a different area of your local park. Allow for plenty of time so that your dog can explore with their nose while you take in the new views. After all, the pleasure of the walk lies in the smells for them and in the change of scenery for you.

Play indoor hide and seek
It's unclear when good old-fashioned hide and seek becomes abandoned in life, but having a pup means the antics can resume. To begin, engage your dog in a light-hearted bout of fetch. Toss their ball or favourite toy and when they scuttle away after it, quickly find a place to hide! A closet, behind a couch, wherever you can fit in a flash… then stay perfectly still and quiet. Pup's natural instinct will be to start looking for you when they return.

If they have a tricky time uncovering your hideout, let out a sharp whistle or a quick call of their name to give them a clue. And when they finally discover you,

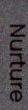
Nurture

Beautiful Everydays

celebrate loudly! Jump up and down, offer lots of praise – and then get set for round two.

Make a standing playdate
Guess what? Dogs and humans are both extremely social creatures, which makes a mutual playdate a wonderful way to spend some extra time together. Whether partaking in a movie night, a hike or a day at the beach, gather up your fellow dog-loving pals and their canine sidekicks for a hangout extravaganza!

Can't get the whole gang together? Not to worry – one-on-one time is just as pleasant and gives both you and your pup something to look forward to on a regular basis.

Make brushing a ritual
Brushing is a soothing way to bond with your dog. Not only does a regular at-home groom result in a healthier coat and skin, it's also a very tactile practice that builds trust in the pet-parent relationship. Lovingly run the brush through their fur and follow the movement with your other hand along your dog's body. Pup will adore the extra hands-on attention and the slow rhythmic pace will bring you a sense of quiet satisfaction.

Cook together
Add a dollop of fun to the nightly task of making dinner by inviting your pup to join you in the kitchen. As you chop, stir and sauté, treat your sous-chef to little nibbles along the way, like pieces of veggies* and other delicious surprises. Bonus points if you toss the tidbits for them to catch. It's like a date with your dog but without the bother of table manners. Winning!

*Keep in mind that not all vegetables are safe for canine consumption so be sure to consult with your veterinarian before feeding.

---

accoutrements

- a whole lot of puppy love!
- patience
- openness to slobber

make it dreamier

∴ Spend time hanging out on the floor for extra contact with your canine bestie; catch up on reading, stretch or relax while listening to some music. This simple action tends to make dogs extra wiggly with happiness because you're on their level for some additional doting. Plus you're in a prime position for close up snuggles.

∴ Watch the faces you pass by while out and about strolling with pup. You'd be surprised how many people smile to themselves after laying eyes on a dog... or even better making canine eye contact. It's a great way to connect with your community.

don't have a dog?

∴ Consider asking a friend to babysit their fur-kid for a romp around the neighbourhood, an afternoon playdate or a full-fledged weekend sleepover. Chances are the pet parent in your life will welcome the break and loving support; meanwhile pup gets a new playmate – you!

∴ Visit your local dog park and watch all the fluffy friends chase, frolic and play. It's amazing how observing dogs running freely, wrestling and being their natural carefree selves can lift one's spirits, make you feel more relaxed and inspire a genuine feeling of joy.

∴ Volunteer with an animal shelter to visit with, walk and care for adoptable dogs. These animals in need will relish the love and attention you can provide – be it a quick brush, a leashed stroll or even some never-ending ear scratches.

pairs well with

Rainy Day Wander | Magical Stargazing | Basket of Cozy

emotional painting

Learning about herself as she grows and matures has been one of her greatest adventures. She's seen and perceived in many ways by others, but is the only one who truly knows who she is. It's a universal way of being that she adores pouring into art.

She most sees herself portrayed in the hazy vagueness of abstract art. The sight of colours trickling into one another; the electric energy pulsing through the different textures; the presence of opposite forces somehow coexisting within the confines of the piece. It's like her aura comes to life.

She creates a little stillness for herself with the movement of a paintbrush. And while she knows she'll never fully make sense of her inner world for others to understand, she can at least seize the blur of emotion and try to communicate her perspective through art.

what's to adore

There's a reason art speaks to us: it is the essence of a person represented. And similar to when we sometimes instantly "click" with another person and feel like we've known them all our lives, art either hits us in a heartbeat or doesn't quite stick the landing.

No matter how complicated or simple the work of art is, it came to be because somebody chose to lay their innermost thoughts bare in an effort to tell us something intangible. How wonderfully thrilling to try and show yourself with only a modest brush. Emotional painting, as we like to call it, is an exercise akin to writing in a journal, except instead of words you use colours to express yourself.

It's not so much about creating anything specific, as it is about working out a mood, following where it leads and savouring the visual journey. Give it a whirl and watch what happens!

---

here's how

Permission to paint
Remember, this isn't about painting anything in particular or creating a perfect likeness of a subject; this is about tapping into your heartscape and running it all over a canvas. So shake out any nerves you might have, drop your shoulders, loosen your fingers, pick up a brush and push some paint around... for the pure joy of it. Experiment, play and let your creativity splatter about freely. You might be surprised how consoling the act of dragging a brush across a canvas can be.

Slip into an artistic mindset
In order to let the mind wander, it often needs a little encouragement to relax. Setting up some music can help to disconnect your busy, always on-the-go brain from distractions and lead the way to a little something we don't do enough of in general: some daydreaming. What would the soundtrack for your daydream be? Tap into your imagination, listen to your inner dialogue and set whatever is running through your mind to the music that is around you. Swirl your paint brush in rhythm with that vision and melt into the moment.

Make it your cup of tea
Instead of using a bland container for your rinse water, why not opt for an adorable vintage teacup? One with a chip in it, if you can, for extra character. It might sound trivial, but something as simple as incorporating a precious piece of

pottery into your painting habit can make it feel even more so like something out of a bohemian storybook. Dab, brush, rinse, repeat, and you're ready to resume your piece with a fresh instrument. Don't have a teacup? That's okay! A pretty mason jar will work just as nicely.

Make a metaphorical masterpiece
After you've painted a canvas, hang it, enjoy the sight for a time… and then take it down and paint it again. Slather thick, rich paint atop what you've already created for something entirely new or add to the colours and textures already present. Suddenly a series of random splotches and brush strokes becomes an eternal layered work of art that is constantly evolving and morphing. This makes for an especially wonderful ritual around anniversaries and sentimental dates.

Create your own artist's uniform
Emotional painting, like our feelings, can get a bit messy in all the right ways, so we recommend popping on some clothes that you don't mind getting bespattered. Keep in mind, however, that an artist's uniform doesn't have to be a full ensemble; a pair of jeans, a flattering poncho or a too-cute-to-boot apron will do! Over time your painting attire will acquire all sorts of unexpected colourful splashes and splats. It will become in and of itself a visual map of your painting encounters.

accoutrements

- easel
- brushes and paints
- teacup or piece of pottery

make it dreamier

- Move your easel outdoors for a bit of romanticism and an open air approach. Whether in a garden, by a lake, in the middle of a field or out on a balcony, soak up the sun while your canvas soaks up your vision.

- Take it slow. The appeal of emotional painting is that a work is never really finished. You simply stop when you feel like it. So if a canvas takes weeks or even months until it feels "done," so be it. Make spending time with a brush in your hand a leisurely event.

not an artist?

- That's the beauty of this exercise – no formal artistic talent required! It's not about replicating something, it's about the sensation of chasing juicy paint from one place to another; it's about the tactile experience of seeing colours unfold in surprising ways; it's about creating a moment where creation is the main focus. Leave your expectations behind and explore what's possible when you give yourself permission to play messily with paint.

- If the idea of tackling a large canvas is too daunting, opt for painting a smaller postcard-sized piece. Or paint a piece of pottery, a sign or even a rock. There is no one-size-fits-all when it comes to art.

pairs well with

Blooming Potential | Meaningful Playlist | Heartfelt Decor

moments with water

The paddle boat gently bobs up and down, offering a mellow rhythm that resets the restlessness she's been feeling lately. She lays her head on top of her folded arms, one hand mindlessly skimming the surface of the lake, dipping every now and then below the cool waves.

The last light of the day is fading quickly. She watches sprightly dragonflies dance along the ripples as watery reflections begin to melt into the depths. Stifling a yawn brought on by hours floating patiently in the late-afternoon sun, she helps herself up and tosses the makeshift anchor overboard. The resulting splash mists her face.

Without any hesitation she stands. Balancing atop the ever-moving waves is a secret skill mastered after countless summers of returning to this shimmering place. She scans the lake, delighted to discover there is nobody for miles to be seen, then quickly peels off her t-shirt and wriggles out of her shorts.

She gracefully slips into the deep blue water and gasps with glee as it envelops every inch of her. It has been too long.

what's to adore

There's no denying that we are all intimately connected to water; after all, a great deal of the human body is water. No wonder we feel calmer whenever in its presence. Always in motion and changing, silky smooth to the touch, shades of blues, greys and greens, and of so many varying depths, water makes for a captivating companion.

Experiencing moments with water doesn't have to mean taking up residence by the beach. Water is a part of our everydays, often in many unseen ways, so it's simply a matter of exploring all of the opportunities for you to enjoy the benefits it has to offer.

Whether it's quenching your thirst, offering you a place to swim, being used to wash your loved items or to soak in yourself, water is a luxury that keeps us alive and grounded.

---

here's how

Sitting near a fountain
When strolling through the streets of a bustling city, there is something so welcoming about coming across a fountain of water. It's almost a way of reminding us that amongst all the concrete, Mother Nature is still present. Take a few moments when you find a fountain to have a seat and take in the presence of the endlessly flowing water. And don't forget to toss a coin in after making a wish!

Mindful moments
There are so many times throughout the day where you'll interact with water and these moments can be treated as welcome pauses to appreciate this vast resource earth has provided us. If you're washing dishes or your hands, take a few moments to feel the soapy water on your skin. The sound it makes rushing through the tap, how it glides effortlessly in between your fingers, the way that it swirls to the bottom of the sink and disappears. Spend a few moments thinking about where the water goes, and how connected you are to this natural element.

Running through a sprinkler
Do you recall those hot summer days as a kid when you'd be sweaty from playing tag and sticky from the popsicles melting and dripping down your chin? You'd quickly find relief when the sprinkler turned on and you joyfully got to run through, not a care in the world. Well there's no reason you can't do that as an

adult! Running through a sprinkler on a hot day is such a freeing feeling. Not really into setting up a sprinkler yourself? No worries – try walking through one when you next come across a neighbour's lawn sprinkler; they tend to soak nearby sidewalks in any case.

Embrace a piece of water art
If connecting with a real body of water isn't possible, you can still reap many of its calming effects by simply looking at a picture of rippling waves. Seek out a piece of art, be it a fine art photography print, a painting or a polaroid and hang it thoughtfully on your wall. You'll find yourself getting lost in its pretty view on a daily basis.

Skipping stones on a pond
Skipping stones is not as easy as it looks, meaning you'll likely need to revisit your favourite pond, lake or waterway to practice. It makes for a fun game and a great practice in mindfulness, because it will take all of your concentration to get the toss and the angle of the stone just right for it to hop, skip and jump across the shimmery horizon. Watch carefully as your tiny stone creates a beautiful rippling effect.

---

accoutrements

- bathing suit (optional)
- towel
- sense of adventure

---

make it dreamier

- For a cheeky thrill, give skinny dipping a try! Find a quiet, private place, strip off and dare yourself to take the plunge. The water may be freezing, but that's just part of the fun! Not totally comfortable with this idea? That's okay. A birthday suit isn't a must for a skinny dip – you can always jump in wearing just your underwear.

- Look for reflections in bodies of water. If you've ever come across a calm lake or a puddle after a rainfall, there are beautiful works of art to be seen. Simply pay close attention, change your view by shifting positions, and oftentimes you'll notice imagery that is waiting to be discovered. City skylines, a colourful rainbow or even your own reflection staring back at you can all be found if you pause and let yourself see.

prefer land?

∴ Try listening to sounds of water instead. Drops of rain, crashing waves and ducks playing in a pond all take us back to the simplicity of nature's soundtrack. If you aren't able to get to a body of water, make a playlist with these calming sounds instead.

pairs well with

Rainy Day Wander | "Anywhere" Picnic | Heartfelt Decor

all dressed up

When she steps into her long slip dress, she feels like a make-believe duchess flitting about her castle, the soft delicate fabric chasing against her heels as she glides throughout her domestic kingdom. Then she pops a few rings on her finger, stacking one on top of another, and instantly feels a little mysterious.

The practice of dressing up for an occasion, be it a ritzy afternoon at home or a glamorous night out on the town, stirs a latent passion in her. It's a combination of assuming confidence in the real world and lusting for a fictitious reality. More often than not, it's as though she's stepping into the pages of a gripping novel instead of merely stepping out for a quick coffee or some last-minute errand. Clothes have the power to do that; to transform any moment into a compelling scene within her mind's eye.

Of course she knows that it's the woman who brings confidence, but a dazzling outfit that is bold, a little brazen and daringly vibrant never hurt anyone.

what's to adore

Have you ever noticed how clothes can transform you and the moment you're in? Think about it. We have a favourite pair of jeans that we love so much we wear them everywhere until they're past worn out. We spend time carefully choosing a graduation or birthday dress. We want to wear something special to a wedding or a party.

Clothing isn't a superficial covering; it's a personal expression of self and can really work wonders for changing a mood. And, in case you haven't noticed by now, we're all about mood. We believe being creative about what you wear and when you wear it can elevate any moment.

Think of all the things you like to do and all of the garments hanging in your wardrobe that don't get to see the light of day nearly enough and pair the two together. The result? A brilliant air of occasion for those small, almost ignored, events that are ultimately stitched together in the fabric of a lifetime.

---

here's how

Everydays deserve to sparkle
Pieces of jewelry are often products of a significant life event – an anniversary, a graduation, a birthday or an heirloom. Yet they spend the majority of the time tucked away in a jewelry box for "safekeeping." What a pity, don't you think? Why not slip on the bracelet you were gifted or the necklace your mother surprised you with on your 18th birthday? Choose a different piece to wear each day and think of that lovely life moment whenever you look at it.

Oh, and by the way, we're not talking strictly about diamonds or rare gems here – costume jewelry totally counts! It could even be as simple as a friendship bracelet from a pal. That tin ring you found at the beach as a child and believed was buried treasure? Put it on. If it brings back a special memory for you, wear it.

Lipstick
It's incredible what a pop of lipstick can do for one's mood – the bolder the better to put an extra pep in your step. Our theory is that if lipstick makes you feel great, why only reserve it for work or formal occasions? Break out a snazzy lip for all sorts of moments: having a date with your latest book, baking up a storm, walking your dog, zipping around town on your bike – accessorize with feeling and add some fun flavour to your everydays.

Keep nothing fancy
One of the great tragedies of fancy clothes is the very fact that they are deemed "fancy" and are delicately stored away for a "special occasion" lest they become damaged. The result? They are hardly worn at all. Free the clothes, we say!

Bring out those skirts and dresses for an afternoon in the garden, sport those vibrant coats to the grocery store and back again and strut your stuff in those prized shoes that you lusted after for so long. Show your clothes that you love them, adore them even, by wearing them over and over again and bringing a little bit of fancy to the ordinary.

Go vintage
Part of the allure of dressing up is wearing something that feels one-of-a-kind and totally signature to your wardrobe and sense of style. Exploring vintage stores is a wonderful way to unearth some otherwise forgotten treasures and make them your own.

Reach for pieces that are bursting with personality and timeless charm – pretty patterns, interesting textures, rich colours… be daring! After all, one does not dress up to look like everybody else and blend in. Can't find your exact size? Not to worry. Simply take your new garment to a tailor and get it altered to fit just right.

Embrace comfort
Resist the belief that dressing up means stepping into pieces that pinch your sides or squeeze your waist. Dressing up is a fun thing (if you allow it to be) and being comfortable is a key ingredient for enjoying oneself.

Look for textiles that are soft and feel like butter against your skin. Opt for flowy dresses, wide legged pants, bright colours, loud patterns – anything that makes you feel like you stepped out of a marvelous story and are the compelling main character. Bringing some imagination into your wardrobe is a fantastic way to unlock your inner creativity and confidence – especially when the clothes are comfy.

---

accoutrements

- clothes
- jewelry
- lipstick

make it dreamier

∴ Pair your dressed up outfit with a theme. Enjoying drinks in your backyard? Break out the cocktail attire. Having a dance party in your kitchen? Bring out a dress that flows beautifully. In other words, dress the part for whatever activity you're partaking in. Not all the time, but once in a while for fun.

not into dressing up?

∴ Not to worry! Dressing up doesn't have to be a head-to-toe undertaking. Keep it simple with one single accessory. Slip on a ring, a bold belt or a fancied hat for a bit of low-key razzle dazzle.

∴ Keep in mind dressing up isn't about the pressure to do so – whatever you wear looks gorgeous on you. This is simply another facet through which to express yourself and explore your creativity if the mood strikes you.

pairs well with

Anything in this book

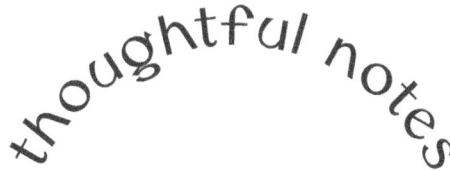

thoughtful notes

Putting pen to paper has been a lifelong love. In elementary school, she scribbled notes on tiny crumpled pieces of paper and passed them between desks when the teacher's back was turned. In middle school, it was often secretly to herself, in her polka dot diary, recapping the day's drama and details of enduring crushes. These private entries were locked away with a key.

As time went on, it was letters on lined paper to her highschool sweetheart, professing her love and plans to be "together forever" – folded neatly and dropped in between the cracks of his locker at school. Sometimes adorned with stickers and doodles on the edges, often with their initials intertwined in a heart.

Then came the years of university, graduation and travel. And these letters became shorter notes, sent as postcards to friends abroad. Each little word spoke of new adventures, keeping friends connected even though they were miles apart. Now, handwritten words arrive in the occasional birthday card, mostly from her grandparents. On the rare occurrence that she opens her mailbox to discover that someone, somewhere, intentionally wrote out her address and thoughtfully sent her mail, she smiles to herself and rushes to tear open the envelope.

what's to adore

Who doesn't love receiving snail mail? It certainly makes us feel special that someone would actually take the time to write to us, inquire about where we reside, buy stamps and venture out to a mailbox to send a letter our way. It's almost like the letter itself is a gift!

Something that used to be common has become such a rarity today, which makes it all the more special. Letter writing can actually have an impact on your well-being as well. In addition to the excitement, we believe writing letters can be very calming and allows you to unwind.

Remember classic movies where lovers would write letters to one another from across the ocean, recapping the month's news that would almost be outdated by the time they were received? Although we may not have anyone writing us letters like that, there's no reason we can't send a letter to loved ones or ourselves, to bring some joy to our day.

---

here's how

Covet your letter writing supplies
When it comes time to write a note, pull out your favourite stationery. Perhaps there's a special paper that you reserve only for writing letters. Maybe you keep all of your cherished writing supplies in a little writing box or desk? Do you have some pretty stamps? Do you like spritzing letters with a perfume or scent? All of these elements come together to create a beautiful writing approach, especially if writing doesn't always come naturally to you.

You don't need a big occasion
Handwritten letters and notes are wonderful to send to loved ones to let them know we appreciate them, to lift their spirits if they're going through a tough time and to congratulate them on a significant new chapter. New jobs, new family members, anniversaries and weddings are all traditional occasions for a loving note to be sent.

But the little non-occasion moments deserve notes too. Send a few words to someone with a compliment, share a memory or share something you've experienced that you wish they'd been there for. Not having a big occasion almost makes receiving a letter even more memorable.

Love letters

If you're in a relationship, writing letters to each other can be so romantic. Even if neither of you consider yourselves writers, it's the thought that counts! Start by writing the occasional love note to your partner and leaving it in an unexpected place – maybe taped to the bathroom mirror or tucked secretly into their wallet. The letters don't have to be long; they can just be a few kind words. They can even be cheeky little notes, because why not?

This small gesture of leaving thoughtful words throughout your everydays can go a long way in making them feel special. And if you're not with a significant other, you can do this same thing for a family member, roommate, coworker, best friend or even yourself!

Find a pen pal

Do you remember making friends with someone new at summer camp and deciding that you'd stay in touch with them by declaring yourself pen pals? How fun was that?! Well, it's time to revisit this idea and put a modern twist on it. A pen pal can be a friend that lives in another country, a senior in retirement living or even someone that you may have connected with through shared interests online, but you have yet to meet in real life.

Ask this person if they're open to regularly exchanging hand-written letters. You can decide how often you want to write, but it'll give you something to always look forward to, while getting to know each other in a creative way! And when you do meet in person, it'll be that much sweeter.

If you'd like, you can also decide to share letters with friends who you see often, just to change things up!

Writing tools

Remember those beautiful ink pens with feathers? What a mesmerizing way to write! Ask yourself if you have a pen that feels best to write with. Try finding a nib or fountain pen to craft your letter for a lovely vintage effect and seal the letter up with some melted wax. It'll be such a treat for the person on the receiving end.

---

accoutrements

- stationery
- your favourite pen
- stamps

make it dreamier

- Sometimes writing a letter to yourself can be a very powerful exercise. This can be to your current self or even your future self. Write about what's currently happening in your life, the elements you love and what your hopes and dreams for the future are. Want to make it extra special? Keep the letter hidden away to be opened at a future date years from now. It might not feel like it now but it will be incredible to reflect on all the change that's happened in your life from a firsthand perspective.

- If you want your letter to feel like it's part of a time capsule, create a vintage effect by trying a tea stain to change the colour of the paper, or try burning the edges with a lighter or candle (just be safe about it)! There are many resources that can help show you how to do this. You can also make your letter unique by decorating the envelope any way you wish – maybe use some watercolour paints, cover it in stickers or even spray with a favourite scent!

not a fan of your own handwriting?

- Go old-school and use a typewriter instead. There are many vintage stores where you can find one. And the cheerful clickity-clack of the antique keys sets a nice rhythm for your words.

- Ask someone you know to write it out for you. Remember, what truly matters is the sentiment behind the letter, but if you can't bring yourself to do it, then find a friend whose handwriting you admire and ask them for this small favour. You can probably persuade them with a cookie or two (or maybe that's just us).

pairs well with

Hideaway Nook | Basket of Cozy | Keepsake Box

more ways to celebrate

- ☐ Celebrate the end of the week.
- ☐ … and celebrate the beginning of the week – twice as hard.
- ☐ The day your furbaby came home.
- ☐ When you've finished a big work project.
- ☐ When you're able to unplug from tech for a period of time.
- ☐ When you go with your gut to make a decision that's right for you.
- ☐ A friendiversary!
- ☐ When you achieve a personal goal you've set for yourself.
- ☐ When you try something new for the first time.
- ☐ When you check everything off your to-do list (and before you go and start another)!
- ☐ Housewarming anniversaries.
- ☐ Each time you choose to make your everydays more beautiful with an activity from this book!
- ☐ When you try but fail (because at least you tried).
- ☐ The family you're from and the one you've made.
- ☐ When you stand up for something you believe in.
- ☐ A culinary triumph, even if it's mac and cheese from a box.
- ☐ A conversation with a loved one that you never want to end.
- ☐ When you face a fear.
- ☐ When a change happens, whether you like it or not.
- ☐ Sunday mornings – especially when you fill them with all the things you love.
- ☐ Just because – you're alive and that's an incredible thing.

nature

We have a secret. There's a pretty simple and cost-effective way to make your everydays better. And that is, to get outside. Just a few moments in nature can have huge effects on your well-being – it can help you think more clearly, relieve stress and allow you to appreciate the beauty that surrounds you with no agenda or distractions. It brings a sense of tranquility when it's needed the most.

Whether it's walking barefoot in the grass, dancing in the rain or staring at the stars, we invite you to discover the joy that the natural world can bring to your everydays. **This is your invitation into nature...**

She'll never be able to give her life more time, but she can infuse it with more *flowers* to stretch the seemingly ordinary occasions as far as possible.

dining al fresco

When she was a little girl she would sneak into her father's vegetable garden and eat tomatoes straight from the vine. In later years she giddily sipped sodas in the park with friends, feeling sophisticated and roguish in the same breath. Now, as a young woman, her fondness for taking tea and sandwiches in sunshine whenever possible sets the tone for her ongoing love of indulging outdoors.

Food and fresh air are the two elements that sustain her most and although she has no tangible proof, she's convinced that eating outdoors enhances the taste of any dish. There's a sublime medley that combines the flavours in food with the bouquet of fresh air, bringing to life an entirely new, complex palate.

She'll gladly take soft breezes and sticky hands over elaborate entrées and crystal glasses any day, knowing the beauty of food lies in part in its ability to nourish one's sense of self.

what's to adore

Everything tastes better outside – chocolate ice cream cones, juicy orange slices, chips of any kind, crisp fresh salads, the list goes on and on. In fact, we can't think of any food that isn't enhanced by the simple pleasure of dining outdoors.

There is an undeniable enchantment about munching favourite foods in Mother Nature's presence. It tends to remind us of lazy summer days, running and playing wildly, pausing only to refuel before charging off on our next great escapade. It can also remind us of romantic fall encounters strolling with one hand in theirs and a warm coffee in the other.

To eat outside is to spoil yourself with a pure uncomplicated joy. You can watch the world go by, take time to truly enjoy the meal before you, disconnect from the usual stress of a day and be reminded that in many ways, life is all about how you choose to spend your time.

---

here's how

Find a landscape
Eating outside is really enriched when accompanied by a view or set against a scenic landscape. Consider putting a table big enough for two in a field, in your garden, under a majestic tree, by a brook or even on a rustic dock. While sweeping vistas are the ideal setting, all you really need is a small slice of green space for your al fresco environment to be a success. Any outdoor area can become your next idyllic venue for the meal of a lifetime while providing a feast for the eyes as well.

Create a tablescape
It doesn't take much to transform a bare, rather underwhelming table into a sensational artistic arrangement. Simply drop a tablecloth into place, scatter some mismatched crockery, add a few blooms, and if you're feeling really fancy, a couple of linen napkins. The incongruity of all these elements purposely not coordinating as a formal set elevates the sentimental energy. A small bite to eat is no longer just a means to satiate appetite; it's a dreamy, romantic affair steeped in allure and defined by simplicity.

Serve fancy, not fussy
Unfussiness is the mark of a truly stunning al fresco dining experience and as such, keeping the menu short and sweet and easy to eat is essential. We recommend finger foods: pungent cheeses, crusty loaves, pitted fruits, dips and

spreads, anything that can be gleefully enjoyed with or without cutlery.

Have some time on a weekend? Drop by your local farmers' market, stock up on fresh veggies, baked goods and jams and your table is instantly bountiful with a local harvest. Keep in mind this is about bringing dining out back to basics in a fanciful way. Make it fun by making it low maintenance.

Find time to escape

Add a streak of spontaneity to the whole al fresco dining experience by keeping a small, lightweight folding table and chairs in the trunk of your car. Then you're free at a moment's notice to pull over to any gorgeous spot you happen across, set up your own pop-up dining space and take a well-deserved moment to enjoy the scenery along with a midday snack.

The best part about taking al fresco dining on the road is that suddenly, that inevitable lunch or coffee to-go just got better. You can take part in a little escapism in the most unlikely of places.

Clean up chic

A final piece for success? A quick and elegant way to tidy up that is equally effortless. For this we recommend a wicker basket. Stack your plates, wrap them up in a tablecloth and place the bundle in the basket. Then use some napkins to cover the cups and mugs and place gently on top. Squeeze in any remaining items accordingly. And you're all packed up and ready to be on your way.

Including a basket like this can assist you in your set up as well, as it makes a convenient way to transport everything to and from your location.

---

accoutrements

- basket
- tablecloth
- mismatched plates

---

make it dreamier

- Invite some besties for an intimate dine-along dinner party. Send them a note and hand-drawn map to dine à la field or beneath the backyard maple tree and include "top secret" directions to the unexpected location. Encourage everyone to bring a favourite easy-to-eat dish and a bottle of something spirited. Then feast, toast and chatter away surrounded by nature and natural ease!

- Dine at sunset so your meal is illuminated by the soft honeyed glow of twilight.

not an outdoor eating enthusiast?

- If getting right out into nature for this sort of boho banquet feels too much for you, opt for an intimate balcony or terrace instead. You'll still be eating outside, but will be a little closer to civilization.

- Dining al fresco doesn't have to revolve around a full meal. Steal the set-up for your lavish coffee enjoyment instead – fewer dishes, but just as fun.

pairs well with

"Anywhere" Picnic | Magical Stargazing | Beautiful Boards

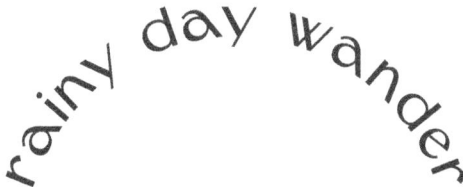

rainy day wander

She senses the rain before it arrives. Something in the air stirs, ever so slightly, and a palpable quiet envelops the usual frantic pace of things. The temporary shift is barely noticeable, gently whispering through the sky before brushing against her skin; nevertheless she's ready and waiting with wide-eyed anticipation.

Rainfall is one of the most disregarded beauties on the planet, a sentiment that brings her a touch of melancholy but also smug delight. It's as though every cloudburst is just for her, showering a heavenly sense of calm that when tapped into, has the grace and power to wash away her worries.

She can hear it now, the rain fervently dancing across treetops and rooftops alike as it makes its way closer. She drops everything without an apology or a second thought and scrambles to get outside. She's eager to soak up the beautiful state and enjoy a variation of the world that most people choose to hide away from.

what's to adore

Why do rainy days carry such a negative connotation? We want to offer a different perspective. The tranquility of everything slowing down, the consoling flurry of droplets ricocheting all around and the musky fresh aroma released by water hitting the ground can all be intoxicating.

We believe that rainy days aren't dreary or meant to be seen so basically as bad weather; rather rainy days, like our everydays, are what we make them. Don't we typically enjoy the sounds of water? Don't we crave potent natural scents? Aren't we obsessed with the concept of slowing down and being more mindful? There's not a more wholesome experience that delivers all of these things more naturally than a rainy day.

Stepping out for a rainy day wander is like stepping into Mother Nature's spa for a little while. You'll return home feeling light and serene, having been doused by a relaxing natural shower that settles the soul.

---

here's how

Dig out a bright pair of rain boots

Wellies, rain boots, galoshes, whatever you call your preferred rainy day footwear, have them at the ready for a torrential excursion. We find that sporting a pair of bright boots is a must to enliven a grey day. Remember, there's no such thing as too loud: yellow, red, even neon pink – the bolder the colour, the better! It's not quite walking on sunshine, of course, but a perky pair of boots does put a certain spring in your step. And while you're at it, slip into an equally fun raincoat if that's your style.

Ditch the umbrella

You know what ruins a rainy outing in our opinion? Fretting about getting wet. It honestly is loads more fun if you ditch the cumbersome umbrella (which never seems to work as you need anyway), and embrace the idea of getting soaked.

Enjoy the sensation of cool raindrops drizzling down on a steamy summer day. Feel your clothes and hair get gloriously waterlogged and celebrate a moment of being completely unbothered by anything. Walk, run, dance. Make your way through the wet wonderland and drink in an entirely different kind of natural world experience.

Do you hear what we hear?
Have you ever stopped to really listen to the different sounds that raindrops make as they fall? Rain on asphalt leaves an entirely different impression than rain on trees or rain on water. Take a pause and take notice. Hear the tinkling of tiny raindrops bouncing all around you – it's like thousands of miniature wind chimes chorusing in unison.

Listen to the water sloshing down the street or bursting from a downspout. Discerning the gentle pitter-patter tones of rain coming down to earth is a great way to bring a little mindfulness and magic to an overcast adventure.

Be a puddle jumper
Don't be intimidated when it comes to puddles. Instead of trying to awkwardly step over or around any puddles that may come across your path, why not charge straight through them? On purpose! Better yet, stomp, jump, skip and splash about.

Are you going to get drenched? Yes. Are you going to shriek in equal parts shock and delight? Yes. Are you going to burst out laughing? More than likely. This bold step forward will land you in a flood of youthful memories and will surely add some amusement to your stroll.

Stop and smell the rain
Some say "stop and smell the roses," but we like to say stop and smell the rain too. Rainfall stirs up all sorts of fresh, earthy scents that you might never encounter if you run for cover every time the skies open.

And while you're out and about in the midst of a downfall, why not take a little extra time to also examine droplets on leaves, on windows or on anything, really. Settled raindrops are like tiny glass sculptures, exquisite yet fleeting – observe them while you can.

---

accoutrements

- rain boots
- raincoat
- sense of adventure

make it dreamier

∴ For those who want to up their puddling game, kick those beautiful bright booties goodbye and dare to frolic barefoot where you can.

∴ Invite your partner or a date along for the fun. After all, there's a reason some of the most romantic movie scenes of all time are shot in the rain.

not into rain?

∴ If you're not quite ready to step out into the overcast world, you can still enjoy the sights, sounds and smells of rainfall by finding a lovely little bit of shelter and sitting for a while to take it all in. Perhaps your local park has a gazebo or there's a covered patio at your nearby café? Maybe you open a window at home to let the showers in.

∴ And while we're personally not true fans of the umbrella, if it makes you more comfortable, feel free to bring it along for cover as you dip your toe into the concept of a rainy day wander.

∴ If we still haven't convinced you that a frolic in the rain is fun, try this instead – wait for the heaviest part of the shower to be over and then head out. You'll notice the sun breaking through the clouds and might even spot a rainbow!

pairs well with

The Art of Tea | Playtime with Pup | Moments with Water

Beautiful Everydays

blooming potential

She wonders if others also notice how monumental moments are drawn together by a common thread – a patient petaled presence. Graduations, anniversaries, even hellos and goodbyes of note are all laced with the arrival of fantastic florals in some way, shape or form; an arrival that is often welcome and wanted.

Flowers are the stand-in for squishy hugs delivered from afar, for nervous giggles that can't break free and for unabashed, boisterous celebrations that party on for days on end. To her, bright blossoms paint cheer and reassurance all at once. They whisper consolations that cannot be fully communicated, they fill otherwise overwhelming silence as needed and they gladden the spirit, whatever its state may be.

She knows that she'll never be able to give her life more time, but she can certainly infuse it with more flowers to stretch the seemingly ordinary occasions as far as possible.

what's to adore

Honestly, what isn't there to adore about flowers? Their vivacious splashes of colour, their cheerful swaying on the stem, the way they seem to embody the feeling of a smile – you know what we're talking about. Flowers arriving at the scene of any occasion always makes for a lovely surprise, but we believe that flowers for unassuming everydays are perhaps even sweeter.

Somewhere along the way, the simple poetic power of flowers became lost and too convoluted – weighed down with endless dos and donts, colour palettes and trends. Let's swap picky habits for picking blooms that we just like and bring more of them into our homes in a low-maintenance manner.

---

here's how

Pick up any bundle of blooms
Pretty flowers don't only live in luxury boutiques. Scoop up a simple bundle from your local farmers' market or neighbourhood florist. Both are easy places to drop by and grab a bundle of flowers – it's a sweet indulgence you can add to an already planned shopping trip.

Once you've brought your beauties home, give them a quick revitalizing rinse in the sink to get rid of any pesky critters that may have tagged along. Then, tidy up the stems, gently trimming them to your desired vase height and remove any leaves that are in the way.

Get creative with vases
Surprise, surprise, practically anything can be an effective vase: teacups, glass bowls, wine bottles, soup tins, mason jars, a lonesome candle votive... the list goes on and on! So don't be fooled into thinking that only a prim and proper ceramic vase can hold flowers. Use whatever you have on hand for sensational rustic chic flair.

Embrace the single stem look
Our natural inclination is to bunch flowers together into busy bountiful bouquets. However, there is a certain effortless beauty that lives within a single majestic bloom standing on its own. Maybe it's the minimalist energy or the fairy-tale allure, but a single blossom floating in a glass bowl or peeking out from the slender neck of a wine bottle brings a gorgeous vintage charm that can't quite be matched by any lavish bundle.

Petal patterns

If the single stem aesthetic isn't quite your style, you can also sort florals in other ways. Try clustering blooms by shape, texture, colour or size for easy, yet dynamic arrangement options. And, of course, always feel free to combine different groupings together in duos, trios or full-fledged medleys immersed in the happy chaos of messy composition. The moral of the story? Don't be afraid to get playful with your petals. Add in green stems or whispers of baby's breath to round out your arrangement and make it more lively too.

Display in unexpected spaces

Don't restrict flower arrangements to coffee tables and centerpieces alone. Bring their bright and bouncy personalities into new unexpected areas of your home decor. Include them in table settings at meal time, on your nightstand, in your bathroom or on your desk. Snugly settle them on bookcases, pop them on coffee trays and tuck them into baskets that you can then move throughout your home.

---

accoutrements

- wine bottle
- flowers
- scissors

---

make it dreamier

- ∴ Ditch the urban flower options and venture into the countryside to pick an armful of eclectic wildflowers from an obliging field or forest (with the landowner's permission if needed, of course).

- ∴ Certain flowers, like pansy, chamomile and nasturtium, can make a delightful decorative garnish for cocktails, cups of tea and even desserts. Sprinkle your flower arranging skills onto your favourite dishes for a dash of decadence.

not a fresh flower fan?

∴ Swap flowers for air plants – a funky plant option that needs no soil, meaning it can be displayed any place a fresh flower can with even less fuss.

∴ Try your hand at pressing flowers. Make sure your blooms are dry and place them between two pieces of crisp paper. Then, place a few heavy books on top and leave for approximately two weeks. When completely flattened and dried out, gently remove the papers and pop your new two dimensional florals into a frame.

∴ Remember also that you can dry flowers by hanging them upside down for a time. The result? Beautifully preserved blooms that will never go out of style!

---

pairs well with

Heartfelt Decor | Brunch in Bed | Time to Toast

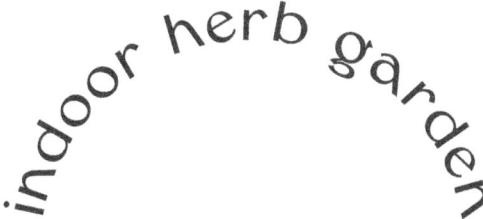

indoor herb garden

Every so often cooking just isn't in the cards for her. The very thought of chopping, sautéing and stirring feels draining to even entertain, so she resorts to a trustworthy standby that has served her well over the years: a simple plate of warm, buttery pasta.

To anybody else it may seem like a lackluster dish. But to her it's a much-anticipated feast because a generous sprinkling of fresh-cut herbs arrives on her plate. The potent leaves permeate the plate with luscious flavour, transforming her under-ten-minute dinner into a triumphant meal.

She settles into the couch to enjoy the outcome of her minimal effort and smiles at the row of lively plants on the nearby counter – her faithful indoor herb garden that is always at the ready to spruce up even the most straightforward supper and save the end of a very long day.

what's to adore

Bringing some greenery indoors is a cathartic undertaking. What's wonderful about an indoor herb garden is that it's not solely about looking lovely (although it does), but also about being useful in one's everydays.

The most basic things are instantly elevated when fresh cut herbs are added to the mix, because their flavour is so powerful. Have you ever had a bite of something incredible only to gasp out loud: "How do they get it to taste like this?" Chances are the secret ingredient is some sort of herb.

Unleash your inner culinary savvy by tossing fresh herbs into all sorts of things from beverages and mains, to cookies and loaves. An indoor herb garden will quickly become your faithful sidekick in food adventures while bringing an added touch of nature to your home.

---

here's how

Less is more
The instinct when it comes to creating an herb garden is to plant all the things, but we prefer the concept of planting only what you love. Reflect on your favourite dishes, cocktails and desserts and see what flavours live within those. Then pair those flavours with an herb.

For example, love ice cream? A dash of fresh mint can make all the difference. A fan of pesto? Basil is a must! Big on cooking curries? Cilantro is great to add to the mix. Choose three to six herbs that you absolutely adore to ensure that you'll actually harvest from your little herb garden regularly. Our favourites? Mint, basil, rosemary, cilantro, chives and dill.

Set as a set, sort of
Usually we're all about mixing and matching dinnerware, pottery and styles. And yes, we do love that look. But when it comes to our indoor herb garden, we equally fall head over heels for a set look. Specifically, white ceramic.

The crisp bright white makes the green of your herb plant look even richer and the neutral ceramics make a gorgeous, minimalist and simple aesthetic that suits a wide range of home decor styles. But wait – we still manage to infuse this with a bit of an eclectic energy by making sure that while all the planters are white, they are different shapes. This adds some visual interest and – of course, our favourite – a dash of whimsy to the display.

Decorate with fresh herbs

An indoor herb garden doesn't need to be restricted to the kitchen just because it's edible. Pretty pots of herbs make a charming addition to any room in your home with ample natural light. Hang them in macrame planters. Pop them in a lush wall display. Make them a table centerpiece or a fun feature in the dining room. Bright green herbs can make a splash in numerous different ways.

Use as more than a garnish

There's no question that fresh herbs make all the difference for many dishes. Fresh oregano in homemade lasagna, rosemary baked into bread, delicious dill in a yogurt dip – herbs go with so many options. But remember, too, that many herbs can be enjoyed beyond the role of garnish.

Basil leaves dipped in melted chocolate make a delightful sweet and savoury treat. Making a cup of cocoa? Throw a handful of mint into the chocolatey goodness. Adore butter (who doesn't)? Add in a sprinkling of your favourite herbs for a delicious new twist! Freeze herbs in ice cubes and serve in your next cocktail. The fact of the matter is that herbs can be enjoyed in many, many forms.

Trim often

Not only is trimming often a good idea because it means you can eat lots of fresh herbs, but regularly harvesting also helps to keep your faithful herb plants healthy and encourages growth. Nip a few fresh leaves on a daily basis to toss into your snacks, beverages and meals. And don't worry! It's not as tricky as you might think.

Gently pinch the leaves at the point where they connect to the main stem with your finger and thumb or use a cute pair of plant scissors. Tending to plants is a calming little practice you can easily squeeze into your day – flex your green thumb.

accoutrements

- plant pots
- scissors
- trowel or large spoon

make it dreamier

- Use individual herb leaves and sprigs to decorate table settings or embellish wrapped gifts.

- Another clever way to use your homegrown herbs is to infuse olive oil with them. Simply pop a generous handful of your favourite herb into a glass bottle, fill it with oil and leave to rest. The herb flavour will slowly infuse the bottle and make a delicious addition to your cooking.

not a green thumb?

- Luckily herbs are fairly easy to take care of. Natural light, water once a week and trim regularly – in general that ought to do it.

pairs well with

Time to Toast | Pretty Plating | Propagating Plants

"anywhere" picnic

The best days were when her parents would make plans with the neighbours on a whim. It wasn't anything formal, but to her 12-year-old self it seemed special because last-minute meal arrangements like this usually involved the awe of the great outdoors. And snacks became lunch or dinner approved foods!

A quick phone call and all of a sudden Mom and Dad were buzzing around the kitchen. Things were chopped and popped into containers. The cooler was pulled out of the basement. The fridge was scoured for anything that could be packed up.

It was the recipe for a picnic extravaganza – and she knew exactly what was about to happen. One too many cucumber sandwiches to be had, running back and forth to the picnic blanket to steal some potato chips between lawn games, playing tag with the other kids, freezies from the cooler that stained her tongue and the feeling of bare feet on the grass.

what's to adore

There's something very grounding about blending in with the elements, which is why we love to picnic whenever we can. It's just a scene of simple beauty and you don't need to add much to make it joyful. It's pretty special to arrive at a location that's untouched, create something beautiful – share food, laughter and fun – and then pack everything up, leaving no trace except for a freshly formed memory.

What's better than feeling the grass beneath you, being surrounded by trees and looking out to the sky as your backdrop? When you're immersed in your environment and pay close attention, you can hear the sounds of nature – and smell them too. It truly is a multi-sensory experience. Bees buzzing around you, birds chirping, crickets in the distance, the feel of the breeze and warm sun kissing your skin and the scent of blooming flowers.

---

here's how

Your favourite foods
Picnics can be extravagent if you like, but they are just as great if you keep them simple. You'll want to bring your favourite foods that can be easily packed and transported and don't require too much clean up. We like to include a combination of one main dish, a few light and crispy snacks, something fresh and a few sweet treats.

We usually pick up a loaf of the best neighbourhood bread to make sandwiches with pesto, and then we get some goat's cheese and sundried tomatoes, along with hummus and crackers, veggies and dip and kettle chips. Fresh seasonal fruit is always tasty and for dessert? How about butter tarts!

And for your sipping pleasure, sparkling water is a great option that you can just add a few berries or cucumber slices to! If you don't feel like prepping food in advance, you can always grab ready-made options at the store, or bring along a charcuterie spread instead.

Pack in a sustainable way
Along with all of your food, you'll need something to pack it in. Don't fret if you don't own a picnic basket, there are lots of other fabulous options. A wooden crate is a great choice, or even a cute tote or beach bag. If you have a wicker basket lying around your house, that works as well! For items that need to stay cold until you arrive, make sure you place them in a mini-cooler or container with ice packs.

In terms of dishware, opt for sustainable choices with reusable plates, cups and cutlery. Any outdoor set you already have will do. If you don't own any, then be sure to stick to recyclable materials as much as possible.

Bring along any other items you might need like linen napkins or reusable forks.

Scouting and arriving at a dreamy spot

By this, we don't mean the spot that looks the most picturesque, we mean the spot that feels right to you. If you're able to, we suggest walking or biking to a local park that you may have never had a picnic in before, so that you can appreciate it from a new perspective. And if you're biking, how gorgeous would it be to place all of your items in a bicycle basket? A crisp baguette, bottle of rosé and a selection of cheeses and pastries. Delicious!

If you're planning on driving, maybe take a little road trip just outside of your city. It could make for the perfect adventure without needing to spend any extra money on an overnight stay. When you arrive at your destination, look for an area of grass that you can settle on, maybe by a majestic tree for a touch of shade, or nestled on a hill for a great view of the sunset.

Make it comfy

We encourage you to make your picnic as comfy as possible. There are so many great ways you can do that. Start off by packing a large blanket or sheet (classic checkered if you like) – something that you can spread out on, along with all the decadent treats you packed.

Next, grab a couple of cushions to take. These can be outdoor pillows or ones you have kicking around at home. Perfect for sitting on or perching up against a tree. Lastly, bring along a soft blanket or two to create ultra cozy vibes (if it's not too warm, of course).

Infuse play

Bring along anything you might have lying around – a badminton set, a football to throw around or a Frisbee for a game of catch. Or if you feel like lounging, a deck of playing cards are also a fun option!

We also love to take conversation cards to our gatherings. These are basically a set of 15-20 questions that you can pose to the group to get to know one another better.

It's easy to make up your own... just tear up a few sheets of paper and write down a question on each – you can include things like "what's your favourite childhood memory?" or "who's someone you really admire?" It's a wonderful way to connect more deeply with people.

accoutrements

- a picnic basket
- blankets, throws, pillows
- games

make it dreamier

- Take the feeling of being grounded up a notch by slipping off your shoes and socks when you arrive. There's something so wonderful about your feet being tickled by the grass with the cool soil beneath you. You'll feel more connected and relaxed in your environment.

- We want you to truly enjoy the beautiful blue sky as your backdrop. One of our favourite ways to do that is to lay down directly on the grass, or on your picnic blanket, and look up. Simple, we know, but it's surprising how little we pause to look at the sky.

- You don't have to have the perfect summer day to picnic. You can also enjoy an afternoon of outdoor fun in the fall! Pack up some fall-friendly food and drinks – like a thermos full of apple cider or hot chocolate, and bring along a few cozy blankets to keep warm. The stunning colours of the leaves and smell of crisp fall air will allow you to appreciate nature in a new way.

nowhere to picnic nearby?

- If you don't feel like you have outdoor options that you can choose from, then there's no reason you can't picnic at home! It's such a fun way to get creative. You can use the same tips when it comes to food, comfort and play, and just pick an area of your house that you want to set up in. Using a room in your house in a different way can make it feel like you've had a mini-getaway, even if it's on the floor of your living room or on your back deck.

- Make your picnic extra special by hanging up some twinkle lights.

pairs well with

Beautiful Boards | Magical Stargazing | Escape into Books

propagating plants

She takes pleasure in the quiet wisdom passed down from her grandmother – that very few things brighten an otherwise forgotten corner of a home quite like a plant stand. Delicate leaves gently sway as comings and goings pass by, while sunlight catches in the glass vases twinkling with water.

There's a graceful poetry within plants, a gentle reassurance that even when weeks start blurring together, life never stops taking shape. And those who pause long enough to appreciate small pieces of the natural world, even if it takes root on a demure bookshelf or a cluttered window sill, can find comfort in that simple truth.

She celebrates her plant fancy by sprouting delightful new tangles of tiny roots. All of the clusters twist and wrap around one another as they jostle to soak up as much life as their tiny presence can. And she's reminded of the beautifully messy manner in which time moves along.

what's to adore

Do you remember planting bean seeds with your first grade class and anxiously waiting for yours to sprout, wishing and hoping that yours would grow bigger and taller than all of your peers'? Do you recall the anticipation you felt when you checked up on your tiny cup of earth each day?

That is the feeling we tap into and adore whenever we propagate plants. And the good news is you don't need to be an avid gardener or plant expert to triumphantly bring more plant babies into this world! Merely harness your passion for nature and reap the soothing rewards of keeping plants in your home.

---

here's how

Rustle up some glassware
Start by collecting glass vessels – and don't worry about what kind. It's incredible how many glass container options already exist from your average grocery store haul, like pasta sauce and condiment jars. Soak the jars in warm soapy water, gently remove the labels and you're ready to go!

Secure a sunny space
Little roots are most encouraged to spring to life when they have access to a bright, sunny space that receives consistent natural light throughout the day. Clear a small area near a window, on the kitchen counter or up on a shelf – wherever sunlight pours in. Arrange your assortment of glass jars within the space and fill each with room temperature water.

Go plant scouting
Equipped with a pair of gardening scissors, it's time to start scouting for pretty plants to prune! Pay a visit to your existing house plants, ask neighbours if you can take snippets from their gardens or talk to your local gardening center or florist about any cuttings they may have available.

Collect cuttings
Carefully take small cuttings from the mama plants. The motion should feel like an ever-so gentle trim of the parent plant. When pruning a plant, a good general guideline to follow is this: cut the plant at the point where a leaf or branch directly connects to the main stem. Wrap the base of your cutting in a damp cloth for transport and then pop it into one of your glass jars filled with water when you get home. It's that simple!

Easy plants for propagating

Keep in mind, not all plants reproduce in water this way. For pretty much guaranteed results, if you're new to propagating plants, try: basil, mint, rosemary, pothos, coleus or lemon trees.

Observe daily

Set aside a bit of time each day to study your propagation station. Watching the growth that starts to occur is a beautiful reminder that change happens constantly. In a few short days you will see fine white or brown hair-like structures beginning to sprout from the stem of your cuttings, which will soon fill the entire jar as a scruffy entanglement of roots.

Your cuttings will then be eager seedlings ready for planting in soil. When it's time, choose an appropriate soil for your plant, fill a plant pot with a hole in the bottom for drainage, cover the roots fully and pack down the soil on top.

accoutrements

- glass jars
- scissors
- a sunny space

make it dreamier

- If you want to keep track of what is in each sprouting jar, craft some charming labels by dabbing on a touch of chalkboard paint so you can write and rewrite on them at leisure. A piece of paper under tape will accomplish the same thing.

- Obsessed with the wacky way plant roots look? Fully embrace the hydroponics aesthetic and keep your plants in water for good. Upgrade them to larger jars of water as needed and have fun watching the roots grow quirkier as time goes on.

not a natural gardener?

- Don't despair! The beauty of propagating is that the plants need very little tending to. Simply make sure the water in your jar is topped up once in a while. No fussing over ideal conditions or fretting about over-watering.

pairs well with

Indoor Herb Garden | Rainy Day Wander | Pretty Plating

magical stargazing

Every so often, the world feels like too much. She carries worries, like everyone, and knows that staying present soothes them. She's known this for decades, of course, but it remains a practice that she has to remind herself of over and over again – feeling heavy for a time, until events ease their clutch upon her heart.

It was her father who taught her how to let go of her earthly worries. When she was young, he would wake her up in the middle of the night, wrap her in an endearingly coarse homemade blanket, carry her outside and point up to the stars. A literal and metaphorical reminder that life is wildly, almost incomprehensibly… big.

They would stare at the sky for hours together, talking and dreaming out loud into space, beyond what earth was capable of. Now, many moons later, she wraps her grandchildren in blankets and carries them outside when it's dark to unlock their imaginations and reconnect with hopeful promise.

what's to adore

We all need a little perspective in our lives. It's alarmingly easy to get swept away by a buildup of worry that then becomes the consuming be-all and end-all to our days. When that crushing feeling starts to encroach, we recommend looking up to the night sky.

For one thing, the world is quieter at night and you can step into a completely undisturbed space for a few moments. For another, nothing grounds you more firmly to this earth than gazing up and out and realizing how truly small you are in the cosmos. For us, it's a reassuring jolt; a reminder that we're here and part of something exquisitely grand that we'll never really truly understand in all its massiveness.

To watch the stars is to believe in possibility, to imagine freely, to whisper to yourself that anything is possible and to full-heartedly believe it, if only for a moment.

---

here's how

Wake up at midnight
Of course, you can stargaze anytime the sky grows dark, but we believe there's something rather enchanting about wriggling out from a warm bed and stealing away into the inky night when the clock strikes 12AM. It's the stuff of legends, storybooks and magic; the whole world is still and quiet, leaving you with only the mesmerizing little lights up above for company and contemplation.

Make camp
Grab your favourite blanket or stake out your favourite patio chair so that you can comfortably lean your head all the way back to fully face the sky (being able to take it all in is key). We love sneaking out with a steadfast lantern or flashlight in hand to guide our way through the dark – a little bit of earthly comfort when hoping to explore the great unknown.

You can even bring a string of twinkle lights to outline your sitting area and make your little campsite feel like a cozy corner amidst the well of nightfall. And, of course, you know us – we never say no to a delicious snack, so pack your pockets with your most scrumptious sweets and treats too.

Watch the sky
This may seem like straight-forward advice, but over the years we've learned that there is a tremendous difference between looking at and watching something. Watching the night sky means devoting your undivided attention to it. Relax your jaw, drop your shoulders, and allow your eyes to sweep across the heavens and devour the cosmic sights.

For those who take the time to watch closely, there is so much to see. Seek out constellations, keep your eyes peeled for shooting stars, chase satellites as they run along their orbits, spy twinkling planets like Mars and Venus depending upon the time of year – and be on alert for other extraterrestrial antics, because… you never know.

Play the impossible questions game
After a few moments of staring out into the universe, it's likely that your imagination will start to creep toward those grander-than-the-brain-can-hold sorts of questions. You know the ones we mean… "What's the purpose of life? What's out there? How big is the galaxy?" and so on and so forth.

We suggest making a game of it! Jot down the big complex questions before embarking on your stargazing outing and take turns answering with your friends or loved ones. Dive into the world of hypothetical and what ifs for the pure fun of it. It's amazing what the impossible questions game will reveal!

Bring some warmth
Even a summer night needs a touch of warmth when you're exploring into the wee hours; it's more about comfort than temperature. Bring a thermos of tea or hot cocoa, an oversized coat that wraps around and around your body like a fabric hug and some extra fluffy socks for good measure. Build yourself a pleasant metaphorical hearth in the middle of the darkness and make yourself at home.

---

accoutrements

- blanket
- oversized coat
- lantern or flashlight

make it dreamier

- If you're feeling extra adventurous, venture out closer to 4AM to soak up the last of the majestic starry night sky, as well as the haunting dawn chorus – that time when the air is quiet and the birds wake up to sing their welcome to a brand new day before the first light breaks.

- Stargazing can be done at any time of the year. Give it a whirl in the middle of winter for a snowy sort of enchantment. In fact, since winters are colder, there is less moisture in the air – the result can make for clearer night skies.

- Keep an eye out for another bright little midnight wonder of the world: fireflies. Make a wish every time you spot one and wish them well.

not a night owl?

- If you'd rather sleep, don't worry! These recommendations can be applied to the fanciful practice of cloud-watching too. A totally different time of day, but just as dreamy.

- Contrary to popular belief you don't have to be in the countryside to enjoy this activity. If you're in a city or town, sneak away to a rooftop or park – and if you can't see the stars, that's okay! There's still lots to watch overhead. Gaze at the moon or follow clouds as they cross the night sky – still magical!

pairs well with

Basket of Cozy | Mood Lighting | "Anywhere" Picnic

random acts of kindness

- ☐ Leave a bouquet of wildflowers in a neighbour's mailbox.

- ☐ Surprise a friend with a handwritten card.

- ☐ Inscribe books with a thoughtful note when you lend or give them as gifts.

- ☐ Smile at people when out and about and see if they smile back.

- ☐ When babies wave at you, always wave back.

- ☐ ... and if a dog winks at you, wink back for good measure.

- ☐ Compliment people you encounter in your day-to-day life.

- ☐ Hold eye contact when speaking to someone so they know you're interested.

- ☐ Help an elderly friend maintain their garden.

- ☐ Carry somebody's groceries.

- ☐ Be brave enough to reach out (don't fear awkwardness).

- ☐ Host an impromptu get-together, even if all you have are chips and wine.

- ☐ Applaud loudly – always with a cheer!

- ☐ Leave notes in public with reasons to smile or funny sayings.

- ☐ Pay for a stranger's coffee the next time you're in your favourite local spot.

- ☐ Hold a hug just a little bit longer.

- ☐ End calls with "I love you" or an inside joke.

- ☐ Bring trinkets back from trips for those who couldn't join the fun.

- ☐ Shop small businesses to help make somebody's dreams come true.

- ☐ Send cookies in the mail, even if they get crumbled.

- ☐ Without notice, drop off a home-cooked meal to somebody having a hectic week.

Beautiful Everydays

closing letter

This is not the end, it's just the beginning. Perhaps you've browsed through these pages and felt inspired to try an activity or two. Or maybe you've made your way through each activity, feeling a bit lighter, calmer and increasingly filled with joy. However you choose to incorporate this book into your everydays, we want you to remember that it's here with you to stay.

Whenever you are looking for a way to create more stillness or return to your sense of self, you can look to this book. Maybe it will live on your coffee table, your nightstand or by your front entrance. Maybe it'll be gifted to your children when they grow older or leave home for the first time. Maybe it'll be passed among friend circles.

Wherever it finds a home, and whoever's hands it lands in for generations to come, we hope that even just a glimpse of it inspires you to embrace the simple moments of your everydays.

Beautiful Everydays is meant to be savoured, cherished and to revisited time and time again. We hope we've given you a window into a slower and simpler life, where you feel at home in the here and now and are inspired by all that it holds.

In loving memory of our Dads, who we each lost too early.

You taught us that living life to the fullest is about the simple, small moments – thank you for this gift.

We carry you with us in our everydays, for always and we miss you more than any words in any book can ever say.

acknowledgements

From Palak

I always knew that I wanted to write a book one day, and I'm so thankful to everyone who has been a part of my journey up until now. This book is a reflection of the incredible people that have had an impact on me in so many ways.

To Mom – thank you to you and Dad for giving me this life and the opportunity for me to pursue my dreams. I am forever grateful and in awe of your strength and courage to achieve anything. Without you both, none of this would be possible.

To Stam, for being the reason I've learned to fully embrace my everydays, and find joy in the smallest moments that make up our wonderful life together (with Bernie puppy too)! This journey is as beautiful as it is because I have you. I love you, thank you for everything you do and all that you are.

To Didi – thank you isn't enough for the lifetime of strength and support you've given me as my sister. I'm so grateful to you, Hemal and Liya for your unconditional love and for always believing in me. I love you, family.

To my co-writer Laura – how lucky am I that you photographed my Embiria launch event, only to discover we share a deeper connection in the vision of how we want to live our lives. It's amazing that our endless hours of chatting, dreaming, creating and gushing over cookies led us here. I'm so happy to be able to experience this together.

To all of my family, friends and community – thank you for being a part of my circle and teaching me the true meaning of connection. I hope we get to share many more beautiful everydays, together.

From Laura

Although writing this book was about dancing in the space between memories and daydreams, it was also shaped by very real characters and I'd like to thank a few of these special souls...

Mark – Thank you for your unwavering encouragement. For a man of few words you always know exactly what to say in the most profound and unique ways. I'm forever grateful for the steadfastness and silliness you bring into our lives. You're the everything of my everydays.

Mum – all my life you've made magic out of thin air and have shown me that love really is in the thoughtful little details. Without these lessons I wouldn't be who I am today. You and Dad filled home with imagination, possibility and whimsy – and I feel the ripple effects of that wherever I go.

Sonia – for your fierce support, dazzling inspiration and "stop getting in your own way" pep talks.

Snow, Al, Jess, Claire and Ash – although I barely breathed a word about this book to any of you, your friendship, enthusiasm, humour and kindness is an essential ingredient to my life. Thank you for always being there.

Palak – for being a wonderful writing partner. It's wild to think that those two young girls who met up on a whim for tea and cookies many years ago would discover in each other so many shared passions and hopes for the future. It's a joy to see our conversations culminate in this book.

And, lastly, Rory and Goose – my darling doglets, for being the best everyday companions and emotional support team a gal could ask for... even when you drive me bananas.

Special thanks from both of us

Courtney – your enthusiastic eagle-eye was incredible. Thank you for your brilliant editing.

JamieLee – for helping us bring this book to life with your beautiful design sensibilities, calm artistry and insightful recommendations.

Tamara + The Fix and Co. – thank you for gifting us with an inspiring grazing board to feature.

And thank you to you, our readers, for choosing to bring this book into your world. We hope that it brings some joy, comfort and inspiration to your everydays.

Acknowledgments

Laura L. Benn

Laura feels most like herself when she's putting words together on paper or looking through a camera. She's a full-time commercial photographer, brand strategist and writer who founded her own studio in 2013 to help entrepreneurs build beloved brands and a creative everyday way of life. When she's not busy with her clients, she's focused on her art career – producing whimsical limited-edition fine art prints, inspired goods and writing about topics that move her.

Laura believes in messy hair, bright lipstick and that even the smallest garden can be the dreamiest escape. She's passionate about helping others turn inspiration into action.

Palak Dave

Palak is a creative entrepreneur, host and author. Formerly an award-winning marketer, Palak left her corporate career to carve a new path for herself. Through her businesses and passion projects, she inspires people to spend less time on screens, and more time gathering, connecting and living life beauti*fully*, everyday.

Palak loves bringing people together (especially over a delicious meal), exploring the world and learning new ways to live well. She has traveled to nearly 40 countries and spent time living in Italy, Brazil, Mexico and the United States. Palak currently resides in Toronto, Canada and is always discovering (and recommending) new experiences!

www.ingramcontent.com/pod-product-compliance
Lightning Source LLC
Chambersburg PA
CBHW040732220426
43209CB00087B/1610